THE
Glasgow
Graveyard

To my ancestor Bishop William Turnbull
(c1400-54), founder of the University of
Glasgow (1451).

THE
Glasgow
Graveyard
GUIDE

JIMMY BLACK &
MICHAEL TRB TURNBULL

First published in 1992 by the Saint Andrew Press.
This revised edition published in 2011 by The In Pinn,
an imprint of Neil Wilson Publishing, Glasgow.
www.nwp.co.uk

© Sally Anne English & Michael TRB Turnbull, 2011

British Library Cataloguing in Publication Data
A catalogue record for this book is available from
the British Library.

ISBN 978-1-906476-18-2
Ebook ISBN 978-1-906476-50-2

Design by Melvin Creative.
www.melvincreative.co.uk
Printed and bound in Poland.
Unless otherwise stated the photographs in this book are by
Michael TRB Turnbull.

CONTENTS

ACKNOWLEDGEMENTS

For permission to take and use photographs: The City of Glasgow Council; The City of Glasgow Council Land and Environmental Services; The Archdiocese of Glasgow; Strathclyde University; Historic Scotland; East Renfrewshire Council; The Royal Commission on the Ancient and Historical Monuments of Scotland; Canongate Books for permission to quote from Alasdair Gray's *Lanark*.

For advice and research assistance: The City of Glasgow Countryside Ranger Service; Colin Mackie (Southern Necropolis); the staff of the Glasgow Room at the Mitchell Library; Sylvia Jamieson (The Ramshorn Theatre) and David Harvey (volunteer guide with Senior Studies Institute of the University of Strathclyde); George Parsonage (Glasgow Humane Society).

JIMMY BLACK (1920-2004)

Jimmy Black was born in Manchester in 1920 to Scottish parents but moved to Shettleston, Glasgow, when he was three, where he was joined later by two sisters and a brother. An East Ender, he lived most of his life in Shettleston and Springboig. As a teenager he had started to write for local Glasgow newspapers such as *The Evening Times* and *The Evening Citizen* but later also worked for BBC Radio Scotland's 'Sportsound', broadcasting poems after rugby or boxing events, writing extensively for television and radio on subjects as diverse as local history, sport and religion, on Scottish Television's 'Highway' and on BBC Radio Scotland's 'Macgregor's Gathering.'

Although a bricklayer to trade his love was always writing. Jimmy had an inimitable writing style and speaking voice. He was a great after-dinner speaker and was in demand at the annual round of Burns Suppers. If a fee was offered it always went to charity. In 1999 he celebrated 50 years marriage with Betty. They had three children and two grandchildren. Betty and Jimmy lived the last few years of their lives at the David Livingstone Centre in Blantyre, Lanarkshire. Jimmy died in April 2004.

Among his many other publications were *It takes a' kinds a getherin* (Edina Press, Edinburgh, 1976); *Yellow Wednesday: the gathered bric-à-brac of living in Glasgow* (Glasgow District Council Libraries, 1988); *History's Mysteries* (Saint Andrew Press, Edinburgh, 1993) and *Eastbank — too grand for a Village?* (Eastbank Academy, Glasgow, 1994).

INTRODUCTION

In Glasgow, death is always fatal. Students of *glasgowness* agree that there's a distinctive Glasgow 'take' on mortality. The visitor making the journey through the graveyards of Glasgow will surely become aware of a special Glaswegian condition — apart, that is, from the common condition of death. You feel it when you start to absorb the atmosphere of the city — its elements of the sad, the arrogant, the courageous, the righteous, the hilarious and the hideous, blended in strange proportions, all to be assimilated and enjoyed along with the weird and wonderful stories of the occupants of those quiet places of timeless repose.

The journey can be a heady experience. It starts with the resting place of Mungo's bones, then passes on to surgeon *extraordinaire* Maister Peter Low, to John Henry Alexander, the actor-manager credited with inventing the Great Gun Trick in which the trickster seems to catch a bullet in his mouth; past the grave of Pierre Émile L'Angelier (allegedly poisoned by Madeleine Smith) and beyond to the headstone of Benny Lynch, World Flyweight Boxing Champion. The choice of graveyards in this book will hopefully catch the fancy and stir the imagination.

Of course, those who plan to visit Glasgow's cemeteries should take normal sensible precautions. Don't forget, while they are fascinating and picturesque repositories of so much human history, Glasgow graveyards are no safer than those of any other city. Always be aware of your surroundings at all times and never walk alone!

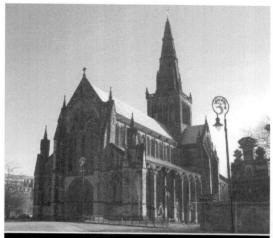

Glasgow Cathedral

Castle Street, GLASGOW G4 0QZ
www.glasgowcathedral.org.uk

We start our tour at the beginning. Centuries before the Necropolis was established as Glasgow's answer to the celebrated French cemetery of Père-Lachaise (which opened in 1804 on a Paris hillside), wealthy or eminent Glaswegians naturally chose to be buried close to the magnificent Glasgow Cathedral, a building that dates from AD1123. A chosen few even had the

distinction of being buried inside the Cathedral. They became part of an exclusive gathering hosted by the patron saint of the city himself — St Kentigern, more fondly known as Mungo. Therefore, our visit to the graveyards of Glasgow quite properly starts

Glasgow Cathedral and Necropolis

with the famous names buried down in the Cathedral Crypt.

It's a typically Glaswegian exaggeration that it should be called a 'crypt'. Actually, it's not a crypt at all. The venerable Cathedral was built on land that sloped down steeply from west to east, so the Lower Church is actually above ground, although at one period it was filled with six feet of soil. However, 'Crypt' is easier to say than 'Lower Church.'

GLASGOW CATHEDRAL

When you first enter the imposing doors of the Cathedral, turn immediately right and walk straight up to the magnificent Quire Screen. Here you can admire the height of the roof, the soaring pillars and the wonderful stained glass. From the Quire Screen turn right, go down the steep stone steps and then turn left again down into the Crypt.

In the centre, under the arches of four supporting stone pillars, the tomb of [1] St KENTIGERN (AD520-612),

3

otherwise known as Mungo, dominates the space. Raised on a platform, the shrine has a richly coloured modern tapestry laid over it, the work of Malcolm Lochhead, gifted by the Embroiderers' Guild in 1973. Lit by spotlights, the tomb with its bright

patterned cover shines out from the gloom. Then, at the southeast corner of the Crypt substantial parts of the original medieval stone shrine can be seen.

The story of St Mungo is an intriguing one although recent historical research casts some doubt on his origins. He is reputed to have been the illegitimate son of Thenew, daughter of Loth, King of Lothian in what is now in East Lothian. As a punishment for her love affair with a young shepherd Mungo's grandfather, outraged by Thenew's pregnancy, had her cruelly thrown out to her death down the southern sheer cliff-face of Traprain Law. Loth considered a shepherd to be an unsuitable son-in-law for a king! Miraculously, however, Thenew survived the fall and managed to escape in a coracle boat across the waters of the Firth of Forth, northwards to the shores of Fife.

There her son Mungo was born. He grew up in Fife and was educated and trained in religion at Culross by the monks of St Serf. Afterwards,

ST MUNGO'S WELL

Mungo spent some time living with the elderly Abbot Fergus at Carnoch in Stirlingshire.

Then, one sad day, when Abbot Fergus was dying, he told Mungo: 'When I die, place my body on a cart. Hitch two bullocks to the cart and let them wander westwards. Wherever they stop, make that my burial place.'

The bullocks carried the Abbot's body westwards and didn't stop until they had to slake their thirst in the burn at the green slopes of the Molendinar Glen. By chance, the animals stopped just below the hill which St Ninian had first turned into a cemetery almost 200 years earlier.

MEDIEVAL ST MUNGO'S TOMB

Reverently, Mungo buried Abbot Fergus up on the slopes of the hill. Legend records that his bones lie somewhere near the Blacader Aisle. This is sometimes also known as the 'Blackadder' Aisle. It is named after Archbishop Blacader in whose episcopacy (1483-1508) the Aisle was constructed on the south side of the Crypt.

Now walk on up to the right-hand corner of the east end of the Crypt, beside the stone fragments of Mungo's medieval tomb. There, by the worn stone mouth of St Mungo's Well, up on the south wall five feet above the floor, a flat gravestone has an inscription in large pointed Gothic letters: 'Here lyis ane honorabill woman'. This refers to a

member of the ancient Luss family, [2] Dame MARGARET COLQUHOUN (d1595), a lady who must have often been sorely tried by the marauding McGregors, as they repeatedly raided her lands, stole her sheep and her cattle.

However, Dame Margaret was spared the horrors that erupted between the two Clans eight years after her death. On Monday 7 February 1603, the Colquhouns and the McGregors had met for a peace conference. However, it soon degenerated into conflict, a deadly clash on the ridge above Glenfruin, west of Loch Lomond. Although only two of the McGregors were killed, some 140 Colquhouns met their deaths!

Continuing the tour, you will see three chapels at the east end of the Crypt: on the south, the Chapel of St Andrew (also known as the Nurses' Chapel, a place of prayer and meditation for members of the nursing profession); to the north, St Nicholas' Chapel, reserved for the celebration of the lives of deceased children (also commemorated in a stained glass window presented by the Stillborn and Neonatal Death Society 'in memory of all babies lost before or around the time of birth'). In the centre stands the Chapel of St Peter and Paul (known as the 'Barony Chapel').

Right against the east gable of this central chapel (but sometimes hidden by the minister's chair) is the shield-shaped plaque that marks the burial place of [3] the ORRS, an ancient Scottish family who owned the estate of Barrowfield. Maybe they could have expected to have a street named after them (which they did), but never in their wildest dreams could they have imagined *Paradise* coming to the easternmost

THE ORRS

boundary of their estate! Well, that's what the football fraternity call Celtic Park!

Going back up the short flight of steps on the north side of the Crypt you will see a brass tablet at the top of the steps, set into the floor and dedicated to [4] MOSES McCULLOCH of Balgray, up Springburn way. He was the operator of a firm of elite sedan chairs – the taxis of his day. Moses died on 31 January 1832, just six weeks before the Reform Bill (which increased the number of people allowed to vote) passed through the House of Commons, so bringing immense joy to many but especially to the people of Glasgow. Ironically, Moses would have made a fortune on the night that bit of news reached the city. With people hurrying all over Glasgow to celebrate this great occasion with their friends, they would have needed transport and his sedan chairs would have made a killing.

Then cross back over to the south side of St Mungo's tomb, looking at the floor. There you will find the person buried nearest to the saint. Wealthy [5] RICHARD DENNISTOUN (d1841, aged 76) holds this honour. Dennistoun owned Kelvingrove Estate which, in the middle of the 19th century, became Glasgow's Kelvingrove Park. This is the park that inspired Thomas Lyle's song, 'Let us haste to Kelvingrove'. It was also the site of three exhibitions and has some important neighbours: Glasgow University looks down on it from the north and, on its southern boundary, the park has Glasgow's Art Gallery and Museum to grace it. By the way, the Art Gallery was built for the 1901 Exhibition. And no, it is not facing the wrong way round! And Simpson and Allen, the architects, did not commit suicide as a result! This particular Glasgow myth keeps springing up like Kelvingrove weeds ...

In time, Richard Dennistoun's name moved eastwards. A huge chunk of Glasgow's East End became the 'wally-close' district of Dennistoun. A 'wally-close' is an arched tenement-entrance decorated with tiles up to about four feet off the ground – and so was considered to be a more desirable and more respectable domestic entrance. Incidentally, one of the claims to fame of this part of Glasgow is that Colonel William F Cody (better known as 'Buffalo Bill') actually did display his shooting skills here, just off Duke Street at the East End Exhibition Buildings. He brought his Wild West Show, featuring Miss Annie Oakley, a party of Sioux warriors and many others, from 16 November 1891 to 27 February 1892.

Now leave the Crypt by the steps. Halfway up, turn left and go down into the Blacader Aisle. You enter a bright, whitewashed chapel. On the left-hand wall, beside the front row of seats, you'll see a brass plate to [6] KIRKMAN FINLAY (d1842, aged 70). This gleaming brass plate reveals just a little about this remarkable man: 'In memory of Kirkman Finlay of Castle Toward'. Kirkman Finlay represented the Glasgow District of Boroughs in the Parliament elected in 1812 and he was chosen Lord Provost of Glasgow in the same year.

However, there was a lot more to Kirkman. In the early years of the 19th century he was one of Britain's top entrepreneurial cotton merchants and sent one of the first trading ships to India. Eventually, he managed to break the long-standing monopoly of the East India Company. Kirkman stood again for Parliament in the May 1831 election. His opponent was then was Joe Dixon of the famous iron-smelting company on Glasgow's Southside – known locally as 'Dixon's Blazes'.

Although electoral reform was in the air, Kirkman was no reformer! Moreover, he became a victim of the Glasgow equivalent of the American Watergate scandal. What happened was that Kirkman Finlay had to secure the favour of those privileged few who were allowed to vote in Glasgow and in the burghs of Renfrew, Rutherglen and Dumbarton. Alas, Joe Dixon's father, Provost of Dumbarton, masterminded his son's campaign. So what did the old Provost do? He took all the voters on a grand tour of Helensburgh, the Gareloch and Loch Lomond, culminating in a wild, boozy party at the top of Ben Lomond. Is it any wonder then that Joe Dixon was returned to Parliament?

Kirkman, whose impressive Castle Toward still adds interest to the sail into Rothesay Bay, did much for the city of Glasgow, but just the hint of a dark secret still lingers over his memory. There were those who suggested it was he who planted the moles to spy on members of the Reform movement, leading to the execution by hanging of Andrew Hardie, John Baird and James 'Pearlie' Wilson in 1820.

On that note it is time to leave the Cathedral. When you get outside turn round to face the south door.

THE SOUTH DOOR

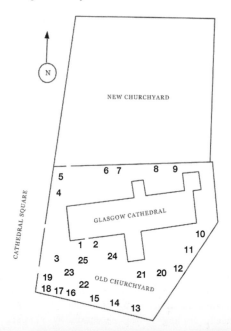

The Old Churchyard

The old churchyard is really much older than the Cathedral, for, as early as the fifth century, St Ninian is believed to have consecrated a burying place on the green hill above the Molendinar Burn. It would be almost 200 years before St Mungo came to take over this 'dear green place' (*Glasgu* in Gaelic) and erect his first timber church during some 13 years of building up the community. More than 500 years passed before the construction of a more permanent stone structure started. Design changes, destructive fires, lightning and warfare led to countless interruptions to the centuries-long building operation. A lot of damage also came from the vandalism of rebels of all kinds fighting for their causes: but the Cathedral survived it all – even the Reformation.

As you prepare to explore the ancient churchyard, it is helpful to use the Cathedral to orientate yourself. Since Christian churches such as Glasgow Cathedral were built with their high altar facing approximately east, the Cathedral forms a highly visible direction finder and a rough compass. By the way, it is also wise, when walking through any graveyard, not to walk alone and always to be keenly aware of safety and security. Finally, remember that to walk through a graveyard you need strong and sensible shoes!

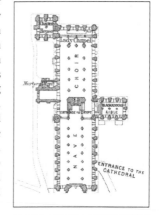

By the 15th century, Glaswegians of substance were being laid to rest here, around the High Kirk of St Mungo. Just to the west (left) of the Cathedral entrance is the classic gravestone of [1] GEORGE BAILLIE (d1873, aged 89). Although Baillie did not regard himself as a Glaswegian of quality, he was, nevertheless, a man of the very best substance.

The great stone that marks his grave is formed like a window – the inscription tells us that he was a member of the Faculty of Procurators in Glasgow, a sheriff substitute in Perth, and that, in the latter years of his life, he used his entire fortune to set up free public libraries, reading rooms and what he called 'uni-sectarian schools.' His stone here tells it all. Imagine such broadmindedness and toleration in a multi-sectarian place like Glasgow — and away back in the 19th century!

George had said that he was doing all these things to 'promote the intellectual culture of the operative classes.' Who knows how many folk read and studied to a fuller and richer life because of George Baillie. A portrait of this remarkable man shows him bearded, dressed in a knee-length black coat, tall *lum* [chimney-shaped] hat and shiny

GEORGE BAILLIE
DRAWN FROM LIFE

black boots. He looks like the comic burgomaster in a pantomime, but Baillie was a giant among men and deserves pride of place in the churchyard.

GEORGE HUTCHESON,
COURTESY OF
HUTCHESONS'
GRAMMAR SCHOOL

THOMAS HUTCHESON,
COURTESY OF
HUTCHESONS'
GRAMMAR SCHOOL

On the east (right) side of the Cathedral entrance, another ornate memorial honours the brothers [2] GEORGE HUTCHESON (c1558-1639) and THOMAS HUTCHESON (1590-1641) of Lambhill. They were socially-conscious lawyers: George founded and endowed Hutcheson's Hospital (1639-41) and School (built 1641-1660) while Thomas gave £1,000 for rebuilding the Old College (Glasgow University) buildings and 2,000 merks to pay for a librarian there. The hospital originally stood in Argyle Street until the 1820s and its replacement still enhances Ingram Street. It provided food and shelter, indeed a safe haven, for 12 old men and six lads who could not fend for themselves.

HUTCHESON MONUMENT

HUTCHESONS' GRAMMAR SCHOOL, CROWN STREET, COURTESY OF HUTCHESONS' GRAMMAR SCHOOL

Life-size statues of the brothers are set into the front wall of the hospital which is now a National Trust for Scotland property called Hutcheson's Hall, although it is not open to the public. Hutchesons' Grammar School, a renowned institution, taught innumerable pupils who have gained fame in many diverse careers. John Buchan, who wrote (among other books) *The Thirty-Nine Steps*, and Jimmy Maxton, MP for Bridgeton, who often upstaged Churchill in the Westminster Parliament – both were Hutchesons' former pupils. (www.hutchesons.org/school/history)

Go now to the south-west corner of the Cathedral. Here, in the grass just right of the path, is a flat memorial stone to the [3] TENNENT family, including Hugh of that ilk who was a brewer of distinction.

To the south-east of the Cathedral, Tennents' Wellpark Brewery, the oldest in Glasgow, still brews on. What would those whose dust lies here, have thought of those famous and classic television

COURTESY OF TENNENT
CALEDONIAN BREWERIES

advertisements and lager cans which once carried the alluring photographs of attractive young ladies? In due course we'll be meeting the Tennents once again at the Necropolis.

Walk north, going around the west entrance of the Cathedral. Just beyond the north-west corner of the Cathedral, on the back wall of the Glasgow Royal Infirmary, a sharply-bevelled stone stands above the remains of [4] COLIN DUNLOP DONALD (d1859, aged 82). The coat of arms on the stone shows a shield, a forearm gripping a sword, a lion, a crown, a ship and a fish. Colin Dunlop Donald was a descendant of the Donalds who were once powerful Glasgow 'Tobacco Lords'. The offspring of the Tobacco Lords were usually given an elegant education and then sent round Europe to learn the social graces by acquiring an understanding of the world. Colin doesn't quite fit that pattern.

He had a sound old Scottish education, became a lawyer and was Commissary Clerk of Lanarkshire. Yet, despite living through a time when the world seemed to be rapidly changing, Colin did not change with the times. He lit his house only with candles – none of the new-fangled gas lighting for Colin Dunlop Donald. He even died in the flickering light of his candles. The family motto was 'Toujours Prêt' (Aye Ready!) Yes, but not for change ...

Next to Colin lies a descendant of another Tobacco-Lording family. The stone for [5] JAMES McCALL (d1803, aged 77) on the west wall of the churchyard, has a spurred boot carved onto it. The inscription reads: 'In Memory of James McCall, Braehead.' He must have been a thrill-seeker: the family motto was 'Danger is Sweet'.

Now turn completely around (facing the east), cross the driveway and look to the sixth stone down the north boundary wall of the Cathedral. What a pity that the [6]

BALMANNO stone by the north wall has been so badly defaced by time and the elements and as a consequence the inscription

rendered so tantalisingly enigmatic. Today, all that you can read is 'Margaret Balmanno, spouse to Robert Balmanno'. One thing we do know is that Mr Balmanno was a Glasgow builder and that the family gave their name (with modified spelling) to what was Glasgow's steepest street – Balmano Brae – that linked George Street with Rottenrow. It is now covered by part of Strathclyde University.

Before the street was constructed, old Mrs Balmanno cherished her physic garden which supplied herbal remedies for everything from gout to dandruff. Undoubtedly her beloved medicinal garden inspired her son to enter the medical profession. He became a doctor in the early 18th century.

The steep Balmano Brae was once a perennial challenge and macho cyclists used to race up it! For a wager at the turn of the 20th century, the ventriloquist and puppeteer, Prince Bendon (a popular performer at EH Bostock's Scottish Zoo and Variety Circus in New City Road) even went down the brae on a bicycle with no brakes! But he survived and won his bet.

Further along the north wall, you may do a double take when you see the most grimly realistic skull and crossbones in the whole graveyard, emerging out of the stone, carved as if they were parts of a real but petrified skeleton. This marks the burying place of [7] JOHN TAYLOR and JOHN ANDREW, humble weavers of Glasgow, interred beside their wives and children. These were among the last of the cottage weavers and would have departed this vale of tears before the mechanised spinning and weaving at the Industrial Revolution took weavers into the 'dark satanic mills'. So, the

handloom weavers, with their fine individual skills, developed over generations, faded into anonymity and oblivion. Nevertheless, the Taylors and the Andrews showed real togetherness, lying there as a family, bonded together in death as in life. And they were clearly determined that future generations would not forget them.

Further along the north wall you will see surely the most mystifying inscription in the churchyard. Carved confidently into the stone, it reads [8] A McKxAB. Was the carver just a bad speller? Or was the 'x' meant to be a multiplication sign indicating that A. McK and AB did a bit of multiplying? Nobody quite knows for sure ...

In the 18th century and beyond, Glasgow was noted for its entrepreneurs, but not many of them actually took their enterprise with them to the grave. However, [9] ALEXANDER SMITH did. Further down, fixed to the north boundary wall, Alexander's memorial is a sight for sore

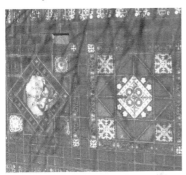

eyes! He was a slater and tiler, and the variety of his wares is vividly displayed above his grave. The memorial is decorated with multicoloured tiles. Perhaps the sales pitch to end all sales pitches?!

Turn right now, follow the downward sloping path and continue round the back of the Cathedral to the south-east wall, high above the busy thoroughfare of Wishart Street far below. Here, facing the corner of the Cathedral, is

a solid block of pink granite dedicated to the [10] MacINTOSH family of Campsie and Dunchattan. It must be looked at in conjunction with the huge wall tombstone further to the south. Talk about 'the writing on the wall' – the monumental masons must have got writer's cramp meticulously chiselling these letters!

This is the final resting place of [11] CHARLES MacINTOSH of Campsie and Dunchattan (1766-1843). Charles was a chemist, one of those highly talented Scots often taken for granted by his fellow countrymen, honoured as he should be by only a select few and usually remembered by the general public for something quite trivial. Along with Charles Tennant of the famous (but notorious) St Rollox Chemical Works, MacIntosh developed a revolutionary bleaching powder that made them both fortunes. He also found a simplified way of using carbon gases to convert malleable iron into steel and, with James Neilson, developed a hot-blast process to produce high quality cast iron. But what do we remember Charles MacIntosh for? Well, he also invented a waterproof fabric – the famous 'Mac' raincoat.

Lying here with Charles is his father, George, his mother Mary and his grandfather, Provost John Anderson (1635-1710). The stone reveals that the Provost was one of those 'dedicated to make offer of the Crown of Scotland to their Majesties King William and Queen Mary.' The Provost's father (also John) fills a place here, and he too had a spell as provost. With Ninian Anderson, great-great-great grandfather of Charles (and wives, children and other relatives) the family gathering is complete.

Walk further on by the south-east wall to what is probably the saddest gravestone in the churchyard. There you can read about [12] GEORGE ROGER Jnr, one of Glasgow's bosses in the troubled 1820s. Tragically, he died aged only 26. His workers (to whom he was a man of principle, virtue and dedication) raised this magnificent monument to his memory.

Come across now to the south perimeter wall of the churchyard and follow it up to the towering and glowering 20 feet of monument to the [13] BELLS of Cowcaddens. Nine Bells were either provosts or bailies of Glasgow. Dated 1734, the carved stone edifice indicates that this lair is the property of the heirs of Sir James, Lord Provost of Glasgow.

Long before then, in 1640, Patrick Bell was also Lord Provost and was delegated to go to the parliament in Edinburgh to declare publicly that the bailies and magistrates of Glasgow were fully in support of the Covenanters. This declaration helped to tilt history towards a Second Bishops' War, but in 1679, another member of the celebrated family, Provost Sir John Bell, fought at the Battle of Bothwell Bridge on the Royalist side, and, at his mansion in Glasgow's Briggait, even went on to entertain the Duke of York (later King James VII of Scotland and James II of the United Kingdom). It therefore seems the Bells were by no means monolithic but certainly knew how to ring the changes.

When the Forth and Clyde Canal was officially opened for Glasgow folk to the north of the city in 1790, the new waterway was a rare and new-fangled attraction. To the north-west of Glasgow, the wee Gairbraid estate was now delighted to see boats and barges sliding past their windows.

Maybe that's why the grocer Robert Craig took a notion to buy part of the estate. In 1793 he bought a goodly chunk of land from its owner [14] Mrs MARY HILL of Gairbraid and Lambhill (d1809), whose memorial is a short distance to the right, on the same south wall. With the consent of her husband Robert Graham, Mary Hill, proprietor of the Gairbraid estate, feued a plot to Robert Craig, with the proviso that it should be called 'Maryhill' to commemorate in perpetuity the name of the previous owner. This Mr Craig did, and Maryhill burgh has grown to become the huge district that we all know and love – famous for having nurtured such jewels as Maryhill Barracks (demolished in 1961 and replaced by the Wyndford Housing Estate but still retaining the original

guardroom as the estate office) and the football team Partick Thistle – founded in 1876 at Partick but now based at Firhill, and known as 'The Jags'!

Next to the grave of Mrs Mary Hill some members of the [15] MAXWELL family are buried. The memorial stone tells you that this is the resting place of one of the many notorious upstart ministers of religion that Scotland seems

to have made a speciality of breeding. The inscription reads: 'Here lyes body of Ye Revd Mr Robert Maxwell who served Chryst in the work of Ye Gospel at Monkton and Prestwick from 1640 to 1655 when he was ejected for non conformity, after that exercised his Ministry partly there, partly in the city & the country.' The Revd Robert Maxwell got the sack 28 years after the famous incident in Edinburgh's High Kirk of St Giles when a cabbage-seller allegedly hurled her stool at the cleric attempting to conduct an English Anglican service in what were staunchly Scottish Presbyterian surroundings.

The sharply cut stone on the wall below Robert Maxwell's

stone marks the burial place of PATRICK MAXWELL (d1623), a deacon convenor of the Glasgow merchants – and his wife BESSY BOYD. They have been here since the early 17th century. Patrick and Bessy had a marriage stone built into the front wall of their house in the High Street which proudly carried their initials. Well, marriages were expected to last quite a long time back then. The Maxwells owned the mansion of Auldhouse to the south of the city, but in 1647 Sir George Maxwell, Patrick's brother, fell heir to the Pollok estate.

A century later, Sir John Maxwell engaged William Adam (father of the famous Adam brothers) to build Pollok House. Then, between 1842 and 1859, Sir William Stirling Maxwell assembled a magnificent array of art treasures in the house. Little did he know that, in another 120 years or so, after Glasgow Corporation had acquired the Pollok estate, another breathtaking art collection – the Burrell – would be housed just across the park. A later John Maxwell became a Glasgow lawyer and cinema owner. He made his name in 1929 pioneering British movies down at Elstree Studios in Borehamwood, Hertfordshire with his new company British International Pictures for which he signed the young up and coming director, Alfred Hitchcock.

Further to the right and still at the south boundary wall, [16] JOHN GEORGE HAMILTON (d1866) is buried a few yards closer towards the main entrance. On the wall his simple stone reveals his claim to fame – his wife was the daughter of industrialist Henry Monteith, and having him as a father-in-law must have taken some living up to.

Henry Monteith (1765-1848) was the son of a weaver (one of six brothers). By far the most ambitious, Henry ran the family cotton-manufacturing factory in Anderston. He was also the leader of a group of go-getting young men who smashed the exclusive right of the Tobacco Lords to attend certain assemblies in the city. In revenge they threatened to throw him out of the Tontine Coffee Room if he showed his face. He did and survived to dominate the place!

When the English radical, William Cobbett (1763-1835) visited Monteith's calico-printing works at Barrowfield, he marvelled at the ultra-modern production line. Henry was way ahead of his time. How on earth could poor John George Hamilton live up to his father-in-law?!

Six paces along the south wall, still nearer to the main entrance, is the wall plaque to [17] PETER MURDOCH (1670-1761). Murdoch was yet another provost of Glasgow (1730-1732). He and his brother, George, who also had a go at being provost (1754-1756), helped turn Glasgow Green into a sylvan paradise – today gradually being regenerated into something of its former glory with the help of the Heritage Lottery Fund.

Peter Murdoch went the extra mile for his beloved Glasgow. In 1745, when Prince Charles Edward Stuart (*Bonnie Prince Charlie*) was retreating northwards after his Jacobite Rising, he ran out of steam and stopped with his army in what was a very anti-Jacobite Glasgow. Undeterred, the Young Pretender eventually managed to leave the city with a load of fresh provisions, boots and clothing for his army. Cleverly, he had held the city to ransom.

After the disastrous Battle of Culloden (16 April 1746),

Peter led a delegation to London to seek compensation from the Hanoverian government for the losses caused by the Bonnie Prince's twisting of the civic arm up the civic back. A lot of good it did them!

You will now be standing at the south-west corner of the churchyard. Nearby, to your right, stands the elaborate gravestone of [18] PETER LOW (b *circa* 1549, d1612/17), surgeon extraordinaire. Dr Low certainly gave Glasgow a shake-up, and he would surely have laughed at the flattering verses on his stone. He was a merry soul. Born in Errol, Perthshire, he was a brilliant surgeon and served the King of France before returning to Glasgow. What a shock he got when he saw the state of surgery here!

He decided that barbers should stick to cutting hair and no other parts of the human body. His plea to James VI for a Charter to found the Faculty of Chirurgerie (surgery) was granted. Thus in 1599 the

DR PETER LOW, COURTESY OF THE ROYAL COLLEGE OF PHYSICIANS AND SURGEONS OF GLASGOW

Royal College of Physicians and Surgeons of Glasgow came into being to set standards of training and qualification for surgeons. Their Charter was the Magna Carta of Medicine! Its authority brought more benefits – standards for public health and medicine and free medical service for the poor.

On one occasion Dr Low somehow offended the clergy of

the Cathedral, and it is said that he had to stand for a whole Sunday at the pillar of public repentance. However, Dr Low burst out laughing during this stint and was made to do it all over again. The Royal College of Physicians and Surgeons of Glasgow is Peter Low's living memorial.

Further to the right, at the far south-west corner of the churchyard, lies [19] Mrs HAMILTON of Aitkenhead (d1616) under a giant tombstone that towers above the path, consisting of nine pillars and much elaborate decoration. Her former estate is now the pleasant residential area of King's Park on the south side of the city.

She was a good housewife. How do we know this? It is claimed that, but for the ravages of the Glasgow climate over the centuries, we would have been able to read some verses here carved in her honour:

Ye gazers on this Trophy of a Tomb,
Send out ane grone for want of her whose life
Once born of Earth and now lyes in earth's womb
Lived long a virgin, then a spotless wife.

MRS HAMILTON OF AITKENHEAD

Let's move back eastwards away from the wall now, to the south of the Blacader Aisle. Its rectangular shape juts out halfway along the south side of Glasgow Cathedral. Under a spreading tree you will find the polished grey granite tombstone of the [20] Revd JOHN BURNS DD (1744-1839), minister of the nearby

Barony Church for 72 years. A stained-glass window in the Cathedral sacristy is also dedicated to his happy memory.

Burns lived in a house just off George Street. His son George was born there and he grew up to own a shipping line, eventually partnering Samuel Cunard in sailing his ships to the Americas. Incidentally, note how long old John Burns lived. Longevity was a family trait – grandson John was made First Lord Inverclyde of Castle Wemyss in Queen Victoria's Diamond Jubilee year (1897). The Glasgow artist Graham Gilbert, reckoned the image of the Revd John Burns should be seen by succeeding generations, so his portrait of the Revd Burns now hangs at Glasgow University.

Opposite the south-east corner of the Blacader Aisle, a flat stone covers the grave of [21] ANDREW MENZIES of Balornock (1822-73). He started a world-famous institution in Glasgow – his horse-drawn coaches were the city's first modern public transport service. He improved on the design of the omnibus

which was becoming increasingly popular, and invented a foot-braking system that allowed the driver to control his horses with both hands. The vehicles, in the Menzies tartan livery, were a familiar sight through the streets of the City.

Menzies was also the first manager of the Glasgow Tramways and Omnibus Company, a forerunner of the light railway with real horse power, which eventually gave way to the electric tram system that nurtured a Glasgow stereotype immortalised in music-hall sketch and song, the Glasgow tram conductress: 'Mary McDougal frae Auchenshuggle, the tram con-duc-ter-ess!'

Move now back towards the west, but closer again to the south wall and directly opposite the south door of the Cathedral. The large ground-level stone, now masked by green moss, declares itself the burial place of [22] ALEXANDER COWAN of Grahamston, Glasgow.

Originally, Grahamston was a pleasant country village in a landscape where hares and pheasants provided sport for hunting men with guns, but this all soon changed. Glasgow's first permanent theatre was built there, and the city sprawled out until Grahamston just vanished into thin air.

The spot where Grahamston once stood is now occupied by Glasgow Central Station, whose bridge over Argyle Street became known as the 'Hielan'man's Umbrella', the traditional meeting-place of exiled Gaels, Highlanders and Irish. Legend claims that parts of Grahamston still lie below the trains, but, alas, successive searches have proved fruitless. Half-a-dozen Cowans resting in this grave were medical doctors. The most famous was Robert, Professor of Medical Jurisprudence (1839-41) at Glasgow University. He died aged only 49 years.

Walk west towards the entrance to the churchyard. The lair of [23] JAMES CAMPBELL of Bedlay and Petershill (d1829, aged 89) is under a flat sandstone slab. Bedlay Castle was only one of his homes. James Campbell also owned areas of Glasgow at Springburn and at Dovehill down by the Gallowgate, where East Campbell Street perpetuates his name. Out at Bedlay Castle near Chryston, North Ayrshire, the terrace balustrade is built with stones from that old village of

Grahamston where Glasgow's main railway station now stands. Bedlay is said to be haunted and certainly some strange noises have been heard there from time to time. No doubt they are made by the heavily made-up spectres of long-dead actors who trod the boards in the theatre that once stood at Grahamston.

Under a tree, 20 metres from the west wall of the Blacader Aisle, lies the elderly farmer **[24] WILLIAM BOGLE** (d1845, aged 84 years) of Papermill Farm in Cathcart.

His mark on history was made when he produced a 'Hiawatha' somewhat different to Longfellow's poem. Bogle's 'Hiawatha' was the most magnificent Clydesdale stallion ever to shake a fetlock!

Now, walk out into the middle of the churchyard, a few strides in from the main gate. Here you will find the grave of **[25] ANDREW BUCHANAN** (1670-1759) a trader in the far-off Caribbean and also with the tobacco colonies of

America. He was one of those men who strutted arrogantly along the Glasgow Trongate past the statue of King William III, flamboyant in their bright red cloaks and white powdered wigs. Buchanan also served a single term as Lord Provost of Glasgow (1740-41). His son George, however, built a grand house alongside Shawfield Mansion in Glassford Street where Bonnie Prince Charlie once spent the night. George named this house 'Virginia Mansion'. The Buchanans actually owned land all around Glasgow, and because of their

link with the United States, two cities in the USA and a suburb of New York share the name, 'Mount Vernon', with a district east of Glasgow (once an estate owned by the Buchanans).

Now, let's move to the north of the Cathedral into the new burying ground. New? Well, it's only been a graveyard since 1801.

THE City of Glasgow possesses a number of equestrian and other monuments of historical interest, one of which is the Statue of William III, erected at the Cross. The illustration represents the scene when in 1735 it was presented to the city that has become a great centre of the Tobacco Trade and the home of Smith's Glasgow Mixture.

F. & J. SMITH, Glasgow,
Manufacturers of "ORCHESTRA"
High-Class Virginia Cigarettes.

SMITH'S GLASGOW MIXTURE
MILD   MEDIUM   FULL

Per **1/-** oz.

Branch of The Imperial Tobacco Co. (of Great Britain and Ireland), Ltd.

STATUE OF KING WILLIAM III AT GLASGOW CROSS IN 1735 WHEN THE CITY WAS A CENTRE OF THE TOBACCO TRADE

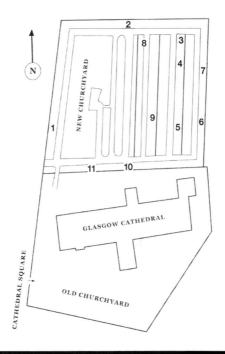

The New Churchyard

Opened in 1801, this part of the graveyard is the Cathedral's sometimes forgotten back garden. Many of the walled graves have been obscured by vigorous green ivy and there has been some catastrophic collapse of parts of the retaining walls, but the graveyard is still well worth a visit. Tucked in behind Glasgow Cathedral, it has the Royal Infirmary towering above it to the west. Part of the cemetery area is also used as a car park for the hospital staff.

The new churchyard is, like all cemeteries, divided into *sections*, in this case separated by three central partition walls, extending north and south. They help to make a place of death and tragic mourning look more like a peaceful garden. To the left, on the west boundary wall, some 40

metres from the automatic barrier into the car park, is the grave of [1] ROBERT EASTON (d1820s), a Glasgow businessman, laid here at a time when the bodysnatchers were doing their worst. Robert's family is also here. Look at the massive metal frame around the Eastons (known as a *mortsafe*) – imagine the sheer frustration of the eager Resurrectionists: the body snatchers had no chance. Even Gabriel's trumpet couldn't move this lot!

Walk to the end of this west wall and turn to the right (east). Here, halfway along the north wall, there is another family of [2] MAXWELLS, this time caged in by a stone chamber tomb. Heavy iron bars form a protective roof above them. These are the Maxwells of Williamwood who intermarried with the Grahams. One stone records that a product of the union was called Maxwell twice, JAMES MAXWELL GRAHAM MAXWELL (d1860, aged 68). By the way, think also about their eternally optimistic family motto: 'I Hope For Better Things'. There is one other interesting detail about the Maxwell estate of Williamwood, south of Glasgow – the father of the late Hollywood film star Stewart Grainger used to live here.

Go eastwards now to the third partition wall, counting down from the car park entrance barrier. On the west side of the partition (at its north end) is the grave of [3] NEIL REID (d1818, aged 32) and his family (at lair No 30 carved in the wall above the inscribed stone). The inscription on the stone tells the story of his son,

Peter, a young bricklayer whom people in Tollcross and Carmyle would watch high up in the air during the bright days of June 1818, as he helped build a tall chimney-stack at Colin Dunlop's Clyde Iron Works. One day, he tragically fell to his death ...

Further south, and on the same side, lies a dominie (schoolteacher) [4] Dr WILLIAM CHRYSTAL (1776-1830). He was Rector of the Grammar School of Glasgow (then located in George Street). In his last years, his old school buildings became part of the famous Anderson College, and his school moved west to become the High School of Glasgow.

DR WILLIAM CHRYSTAL, COURTESY OF THE HIGH SCHOOL OF GLASGOW

Chrystal was sent in to take over the Grammar School after its teaching standards had been described as 'shoddy' and soon transformed it into a lustrous lyceum of learning! The Anderson College, of course, vanished to make way for the Glasgow Royal Technical College which, in 1964, became the University of Strathclyde. William Chrystal would surely have been proud to know that his old Grammar School, renamed the High School, would produce two Prime

Ministers – Liberal Sir Henry Campbell-Bannerman (1836-1908), and Tory Andrew Bonar Law (1858-1923).

Some metres to the south is the stone of the Italian carver and gilder and barometer maker [5] ANTONIO GALLETTI (fl.1798-1858). Many industrious Italians came to Glasgow around the middle of the 19th century and set about the glorious mission of energising Glasgow's tastebuds with delicious ice cream and nutritious fish suppers. Such superb cuisine remains a firm favourite in the local diet – in spite of the arrival of newer exotica. But there were Italians here long before the advent of those bearing potato chips and pokey-hats.

ORNAMENTAL PLASTER, COURTESY OF THE CORNICE MUSEUM, PEEBLES

Antonio Galletti arrived here along with many other skilled European artists and craftsmen. They were brought in by wealthy Glasgow merchants who wanted their mansions to be as splendid as those in London, Paris or Rome. These immigrant painters, sculptors, plasterworkers, woodcarvers and gilders were master craftsmen whose rich decorative work may still be seen, for instance, at Lauriston House in Carlton Place. In Antonio Galletti's case, he loved

Glasgow so much that he exchanged the warm, Mediterranean breezes for the chilling airs of Glasgow for the rest of his life.

One of Glasgow's finest architects [6] DAVID HAMILTON (1768-1843) must have cherished skills such as Galletti's. Over on the east boundary wall, towards the south corner, bold lettering above his lair declares: 'The Property of David Hamilton, Architect'. Hamilton designed Hutchesons' Hall in Ingram Street, and re-designed the

house of the Tobacco Lord William Cunninghame in Queen Street, turning it into the Royal Exchange. Today it is the Gallery of Modern Art. His extensions to Hamilton Palace were acclaimed, and his design for the new House of Commons won an award but was not the final choice. Nevertheless, Hamilton seems to have been a very modest man with a sunny disposition. He had a wide circle of friends with whom he often enjoyed, as Glasgow folk do, a *rerr* (rare) laugh!

Just a bit further north on this path and by the east boundary wall, are the broken remains of a red granite memorial stone to the [7] Revd JOHN ROXBURGH DD (1806-80). Roxburgh was one of the stout souls who led their congregations out of the Church of Scotland during the 1843 Disruption

and into the new Free Church. In 1845, he and his congregation built their own church, Free St John's.

Later they united with Renfield Church in Renfield Street. Their church has long since gone, but the name 'St John's' survives. As for St John's Renfield Church, it's alive and well and working way out west at Kelvindale. Somewhere under the rubble is also a sad little memorial. Mr Roxburgh's descendant, **ROBERT ROXBURGH** (d1916, aged 19), a midshipman, died on board HMS *Indefatigable*, sunk on 31 May 1916 at the Battle of Jutland.

Now, let's go up to the north end of the middle path. Many 19th-century Glasgow folk saw things more clearly after they had made the acquaintance of [8] **WILLIAM McKENZIE** (d1868, aged 77), now buried under a memorial stone on the west side of the centre path, right at the north end. McKenzie was the first lecturer in Ophthalmology at Glasgow University. He edited the *Glasgow Medical Journal*, undertook extensive research into diseases of the eye, and was a co-founder of the Glasgow Eye Infirmary. He numbered Queen Victoria among his many distinguished patients.

South from McKenzie's grave — about halfway down the path and on the east side — you will find a huge granite block that marks the last resting place of a man who had a choice of surnames. The mysterious [9] **JAMES McORAN** or **CAMPBELL** (d1831) came from near the Lake of Menteith in Perthshire but died in Glasgow. A cloud of mystery hangs over that name, 'McOran'. A

Campbell forebear of James, back in the 17th century, committed some misdemeanour. Instead of concealing his identity behind a false moustache and glasses, he simply changed his name from Campbell to McOran.

The Campbells eventually outlived the disgrace and then dropped the name, McOran. The names of Sir James Campbell and William Campbell are also here and they were certainly men of substance. Sir James was Lord Provost of Glasgow (1840-3) and he and William were successful drapery businessmen, William in particular being a saintly soul who married a lady described as 'the lovely Miss Roxburgh'. Their wedding was a splendid affair of Hollywood proportions, but it is not recorded if brother James was the best man.

Both men had strong social awareness and did much to relieve the effects of poverty in the city. James had a son called Henry. This lad married the daughter of a rich Manchester wholesaler, included her name in his by deed poll, and thus became Sir Henry Campbell-Bannerman, the first Glasgow man to be Prime Minister.

By the way, do you remember William McKenzie, the eye doctor? A colleague of his lies down by the south boundary wall. The memorial on it to [10] Dr HARRY RAINY (1792-1876), is placed on nearly the middle of the wall. There are quite a few words of comfort taken from the Bible on this stone — three texts in all. Dr Harry was a surgeon at the Eye Infirmary in Willie McKenzie's time, but, being a really versatile man, he was also Professor of Jurisprudence at the University.

DR HARRY RAINY,
COURTESY OF
GLASGOW UNIVERSITY

Nearer to the new graveyard automatic barrier, by the south wall, a flat stone covers the grave of [11] WILLIAM RIDDELL (d1832). He must have been one of the first railway contractors in Scotland. William died at Broomfield in Springburn, just a year after the opening of Scotland's first railway to carry steam locomotives – the Glasgow and Garnkirk. Could he have guessed that one day Springburn would become locomotive-builder to the world? Maybe not ...

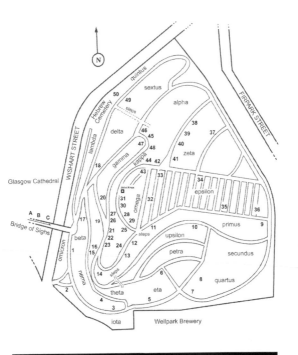

The Glasgow Necropolis

Cathedral Square

The management rules of the Necropolis are available from:

**Glasgow City Council, Chief Executive's Office,
City Chambers, George Square, Glasgow G2 1DU
Tel: 0141 287 5064**

I n his *Necropolis Glasguensis: Thoughts on Death and Moral Stimulus* (1831), the Glasgow City Chamberlain and writer John Strang (1795-1863) presented his vision of creating a central city cemetery for Glasgow on the grand scale.

THE NECROPOLIS, COURTESY OF RCAHMS

The inspiration behind Strang's vision was the living nightmare of death and disease that continuously afflicted the city. In the early 1800s, some 5000 people – mostly Irish and Highland migrants – died every year in the city from cholera, typhus or other fever epidemics. As there was nowhere else to dispose of the bodies, they were buried to the north of the Cathedral, in large pits behind the old Royal Infirmary. The stench must have been appalling.

John Strang fervently believed that Glasgow's citizens would want their last resting place to be in a bright, flowery haven of peace. The Fir Park, a hill on the other side of the Molendinar Burn from the Cathedral hill, seemed to be the ideal location.

Delighted by Strang's proposal, and as the trees in Fir Park had long since vanished, Lord Provost James Ewing sold the hill to his Merchant colleagues, and the project was put into effect. A design competition for the new cemetery brought an eager response from a number of prominent architects.

The winner was John Bryce, who based his design on the elegant Père-Lachaise cemetery in Paris. The 17 hectares of the prestigious Parisian graveyard opened in 1804 on a hill that had previously been pleasure gardens, laid out with paths and trees. So Fir Park was slowly turned into a pleasure garden enhanced by graceful elms and weeping willows. This peaceful layout helped make John Strang's vision come true. Scotland's first 'hygienic' graveyard was becoming a reality, and would be special in another way. It would be

PÈRE-LACHAISE CEMETERY, PARIS

open to people of all faiths – Catholics, Jews, Protestants ... even those who professed no faith at all. However, although the new burial ground was intended to be multi-faith, it soon acquired an unmistakeable symbol of how Glasgow's Presbyterianism had taken root.

THE NECROPOLIS IN ITS EARLY SPLENDOUR

In 1825 the foundation was laid for a gigantic pillar that would support a 12-foot statue of John Knox (c1514-72), the former Roman Catholic papal notary and leading figure of the Protestant Reformation. The statue's stone head would tower some 70 metres above sea level. Once erected, Robert Forrest's carving of Knox stood in almost total isolation on top of its 18-metre Doric column for a year or two, scowling his disapproval at the City's miscreants. Today, under his flat Geneva bonnet, Knox still keeps a weather eye on Glasgow from his hilltop!

THE STATUE OF JOHN KNOX, COURTESY OF GLASGOW CITY COUNCIL LAND AND ENVIRONMENT SERVICES

Work on the Necropolis was fairly well advanced by September 1832, enough to allow the first burial. This came through an offer from the city Synagogue to purchase a burial place for the use of Glasgow's Hebrew congregation. Thus Joseph Levi, former quill merchant and a victim of cholera, was laid to rest that September, the first tenant in Glasgow's new City of the Dead. The following year the Necropolis officially opened, with the splendid stone bridge over the Molendinar Glen creating an imposing approach-road. St Mungo's legendary Molendinar Burn still flowed with solemn gurgle far below, so Glasgow (being full of scholars, lovers of classical learning and of Italian, and especially Venetian, culture) almost immediately renamed the Necropolis entrance as the 'Bridge of Sighs' in dubious homage to Venice's *Ponte dei Sospiri*, the covered bridge which connected the Doge's prisons to the inquisitor's rooms. Today, however, the Molendinar Burn is no more than a culvert, a covered water-channel under the busy thoroughfare of Wishart Street – a road that occupies most of the space of the former Glen.

In due course, its eminence as a Glasgow landmark even

GLASGOW CATHEDRAL,
THE BRIDGE OF SIGHS
AND WISHART STREET

made the Necropolis a literary icon. In his novel *Lanark* (Canongate Books, 1969) the Scottish writer Alasdair Gray most evocatively describes the Necropolis under snow. He imagines his main character being swallowed up by a speaking mouth that emerges out of the earth among the tombstones, pronouncing the double-edged statement that 'I am the way out!'

To the passing visitor the maze-like appearance of the Necropolis is instantly intriguing. With its half-hidden monuments, obscured by trees and bushes, it has the veiled mystery of a medieval allegorical fantasy. Even before you enter its gates the view from Cathedral Square (at the north side of the 'Bridge of Sighs') presents an unnerving skyline of bewildering architectural style and detail emerging above the trees. And some of Glasgow's best architects produced their finest memorials here: John Baird (who designed Jamaica Street's Iron Building); 'Greek' Thomson (whose churches still grace the city); Charles Wilson (designer of Park Circus) and JT Rochead (who designed the Wallace Monument on Stirling's Abbey Craig).

To begin our tour of the Necropolis, walk through the imposing cast-iron black and gold gates. Just after you pass through the gates, look to your left. Here is a grassy area with paving and a small heart-shaped pink granite stone [A]. Surrounded by

toys, it is one of five memorial gardens established by the City of Glasgow Council since 1995 in response to families who have lost children, either through stillbirth, or as neonatal mortalities or of deaths in infancy, all of which today still form a regrettably significant statistic. The City Council, having been approached by families in mourning for their tragically early bereavement, decided to set up this city centre memorial garden at the Necropolis in place of the usual communal plot for such deaths as a way of returning grieving back to the control of the parents.

Further down the road from the entrance and still on the left-hand side, is a recently erected memorial [B] to the 29 servicemen from the Glasgow area (or who are buried in Glasgow) who were awarded the Victoria Cross. Further down again is [C] a memorial to those who lost their lives during the Korean War. The British Korean Veterans monument, with its grey granite stone and two granite seats, commemorates those servicemen and women who died between June 1950 and July 1953.

Now walk over the Bridge of Sighs with the traffic of Wishart Street below your feet and enter the welcoming precincts of Glasgow's Necropolis, City of the Dead. Look straight over the bridge at the grandiose and muscular red sandstone entrance façade bolted into the hillside. It has a dark and

mysterious central chamber, with smaller side openings and a sturdy pillar supporting each end. In reality, it only covers a tiny cave where cemetery equipment is stored. However, it was built with quite other purposes in mind – the Merchants of Glasgow planned to drive a series of passages right through the rock to create hidden catacombs for Glasgow's wealthy dead and so keep them safe from the body snatchers who tried to sell bodies to the anatomists for medical research. However, the Anatomy Act of 1832 stopped the grave robbers in their tracks and the Merchants' plan was never needed – the cave is all that is left of the project. Nevertheless, it was, at one time, used as a temporary holding area for bodies awaiting final interment. The Egyptian Vault south of John Knox's statue was also designed for this purpose.

Now a little geology! The City of Glasgow is built on a group of mounds (known as *drumlins*). The Necropolis was constructed on a drumlin whose steep slopes and irregular shape makes it impossible to design a neat, square layout of paths such as was possible at the Père-Lachaise cemetery in Paris. Instead, the paths of the Necropolis twist and crisscross in tight and tortuous spirals winding up on the side of hill, eventually achieving a more regular grid formation at the plateau on the summit. Because of this topographical irregularity, the task of locating the site of individual graves may not always be easy and often takes a lifetime of searching and study. However, the planners divided the Necropolis into separate *sections*, each identified by a letter of the Greek alphabet (*alpha, beta*) or a Latin numeral (*primus, secundus*).

Armed with this ground plan which can be interpreted by grave numbers and sections, the intrepid (and sensibly shod) explorer will, with some determined detective work, in time uncover the myriad fascinations of this extraordinary mountain of memories – at times as disturbing as Peter Breugel's awesome painting of 'The Tower of Babel', at others as extravagantly decorative as a many layered wedding-cake!

Remembering that the Cathedral is orientated approximately east-to-west (that its sanctuary faces east), the visitor can follow compass directions by referring back to the Cathedral as a direction finder. In other words, when walking over the Necropolis, the Cathedral can often function as an easily visible compass.

Having crossed the 'Bridge of Sighs', turn right. Fifty paces along the main pathway (in the *Mnema* section), look left to a stone just in front of a wall. Here lies [1] WILLIAM HARPER MINNOCH (1820-83) who lived in fashionable Blythswood Square during the 1850s. His story is not unique: he fell in love with the girl next door. Their friends and relations were delighted about this romance, but, ah, love was destined to be blighted. William's girlfriend was arrested and

tried for the murder of another lover – but enough of this. The full story will be revealed later when we visit St David's (*Ramshorn*), another of the city's graveyards.

Keep walking along the main pathway, still with the Bridge of Sighs to your back, on down into the Iota section, turning right down towards the gate that opens into Wishart Street. But just before you reach the gate, take the path that swings up to your left. As you walk, count the gravestones on your right-hand side and then stop at the 14th stone. In this graveyard of imposing and grandiose memorials, this is a relatively modest one: a stone with a curved top dedicated to [2] CHARLES WILLIAM FRY (1838-82).

In 1880, William Booth, founder of the Salvation Army, declared that 'Secular music, do you say, belongs to the devil? Does it? Well, if it did I would plunder him for it, for he has no right to a single note.' Charles Fry made sure he didn't. He was the Salvation Army's first bandmaster but died in Polmont at a relatively young age.

Continue along the path where you see Tennent's Wellpark Brewery looming up at you, belching clouds of steam, its churning cooling plant resembling a huge science-fiction space station.

TENNENT'S WELLPARK BREWERY

Carry on round the bend on this path, back into the *Mnema* section and, opposite the brewery's silver tanks, look out on your left for the very tall grey-green obelisk that marks the burial plot of the painter [3] JAMES MITCHELL (d1873, aged 71). What is so remarkable about his resting place and that of his family is that his parents' house once stood on this very spot. Indeed, the Mitchell

grandfather resided there before them — there were Mitchells living here for more than half a century. How apt that James Mitchell should rest beneath his childhood home, the joys of which are extolled in verses on the stone.

Now make a sharp left U-turn up onto the newly laid tarmac path that rises to a level above where Willie Minnoch is buried. Walk 50 paces from where the hairpin turn is made. Keep on the grassy path in front of you, but do not take the other path that also rises up. Below you on your left (still in *Mnema*) you will see a weather-beaten stone that continues to remind the world of [4] ALEXANDER RODGER (b1784, died in his 60s), known as 'Sandy' to his pals.

Sandy Rodger was born in Mid Calder, West Lothian but moved to Glasgow in 1846. He became a comic poet, taking particular pleasure in embarrassing polite society. When George IV visited a tartan-swathed Edinburgh in 1822, Sir Walter Scott celebrated the occasion with a solemn poem, 'Carle, now the King's come'. Sandy Rodger, on the other hand, marked the occasion with an irreverent parody!

Sandy was a Radical weaver and suffered for it. Sedition was in the air. The police broke into his house and discovered irrefutable evidence of his guilt! The poet's bible was lying open at the Second Book of Samuel — the passage that clearly spelled out the duties of kings. So Sandy was thrown into jail, but, happily, released soon after. Perhaps he drove his gaolers mad by reciting his poems. Sandy's headstone records that he was a man gifted with feeling, humour and fancy.

Turn back now and retrace your steps again onto the main roadway, to the *Theta* section — opposite the Wellpark Brewery. Pass the edge of the old wall on your right and follow the retaining stone wall to your left. Now look carefully out to your left for a tall and magnificent Celtic cross of grey granite in memory of [5] ALEXANDER McCALL (d1888, aged 52). Chief Constable of Glasgow for 18 years, McCall was in charge through some very rough times in the city's history. He died just as Glasgow opened its imposing City Chambers. McCall's profile in bronze complements the fine detail of the stone cross. Incidentally, there is something special about this monument — it was designed by the ingenious and fashionable architect Charles Rennie Mackintosh.

ALEXANDER McCALL, COURTESY OF STRATHCLYDE POLICE

Continue straight forward in an easterly direction for about 60 paces, following the direction of the low stone wall on your left as it rises up along the path. Then turn to your right (into the *Eta* section) and look for a small, plain stone in front of you which leans back at a sharp angle under a tree.

It is capped with green ivy and marks the grave of [6] HUGH PERCY FORSTER, Paymaster of Her Majesty's 63rd Regiment of Foot. That little stone reveals much of Lieutenant Forster's family history. He was one of 11 brothers, 'nine of whom devoted their lives and services to their country in the Peninsular War [1808-14]'. That War also brought fame to Glasgow's General Sir John Moore (1761-1809) who defeated Napoleon's army at Corunna in Galicia, Western Spain. Sadly he died after being hit by a cannonball, in the hour of victory.

History might have taken a very different course if Moore and Napoleon's paths had crossed earlier. Napoleon was in his native Corsica round about 1790 when Pasquale Paoli, the Corsican patriot, threw the French out of his island. British troops backed Paoli and, as a reward, Britain was allowed to rule Corsica (1794-96). Napoleon weighed the situation up and, in 1793, decided to join the French. Coincidentally, who should arrive on the island just one year later? None but a 32-year-old British officer named John Moore.

It is intriguing to speculate what might have happened if Napoleon had stayed in Corsica and had met John Moore. The two great soldiers might have become friends. Moore might have persuaded Napoleon to take a commission in the British Army. There might never have been a Battle of Corunna, and no Forster brothers on the Iberian Peninsula.

Now go over the grass to the path in front of the tall Brewery chimney. Turn right and then left (into the *Quartus* section). In the second row of stones – the second-last stone at the end of the row – lies the Mannheim-born musician [7] ROBERT HECKMANN (1849-87) with four bars of a musical quotation from the works of Beethoven – and a comment written on the finale of his String Quartet in F Major, Op. 135 'Must it be? It must! It must be!'. Halfway further along the same row of stones yet more bars of music can be found on the memorial to [8] JOHN BELL (1823-56). Bell was born in Gourock but died in Trinidad. The words on the stone are: 'Angels beckon me to the Land o' the Leal ' from 'The Land o' the Leal [loyal]', a song written by Lady Carolina Nairne (1766-1845).

Pause a minute and reflect on what you see about you, and what you do not see. It is believed that somewhere about here, in a vast communal grave, were buried the 19th-century victims of Glasgow's many virulent fevers.

Keep going along the grassy path you are on, then turn left and north (up into the *Primus* section), following the pathway as it curves up to your right towards the plateau above. At the end of the row of stones look two rows behind. Here you will find a heart-shaped stone lying flat in the grass under your feet. Here is buried the distinguished naval architect [9] GEORGE LENNOX WATSON (1851-1904) who

was called to eternity in the middle of a busy life, after he had designed hundreds of racing yachts for lesser beings, as well as his most prestigious project, the royal yacht, *Britannia,* for Edward VII. Today, his stone still catches the sun, as his yachts once did, although the salty gusts of the sea are now replaced by the more balmy breezes of the modern Merchant City.

With such heady thoughts in mind, turn back down to the west again, towards Wishart Street and the Cathedral. Retrace your steps down the pathway but keep going straight ahead (into the *Upsilon* section), with the high rock-face of the old Ladywell Quarry rising to your right. From the tall obelisk at the corner of the path on your left, walk westwards to the 19th grave on your left (another obelisk) and then look behind the front row of graves at a stone in the grass that faces towards the brewery.

You will see a stone inscribed to the memory of [10] JOHN McDONALD (d1882, aged 52), a Glasgow Post Office letter carrier, a humble 'postie' who delivered good news and bad, in sunshine and in showers. In 1840, when the Penny Post service was first introduced, John was only ten years old. At that time people were still getting used to the idea of licking stamps, as James Chalmers of Dundee had only invented the adhesive stamp six years before. Incidentally, being described as 'the late' letter carrier is merely a reference to the fact that he is deceased and not a reflection on John's time-keeping!

Head along the path with the *Petra* section on your left and there (still in *Upsilon*), sheltered in a rugged cranny of the rock face (just under the steps) is the pink granite obelisk erected to generations of the [11] TENNENT family. Among

COURTESY OF TENNENT CALEDONIAN BREWERIES

those buried here is CHARLES SP TENNENT (d1864, aged 47). This family certainly kept very close to their place of business – the Tennent monument

still looks down on Tennent's busy Wellpark Brewery. The Tennent ancestors would no doubt be amazed by the state-of-the-art technology which today produces the beer and lager in a

COURTESY OF TENNENT CALEDONIAN BREWERIES

foaming flood beyond their most fermented dreams.

Ignore the steps zigzagging up to your right. Walk forward again: to your right, a little further on, still in *Upsilon*, past the red eye-catching but rusted Gothic cast-iron monument to [12] ALEXANDER MACKENZIE (d1875, aged 62), a Merchant of the City of Glasgow. Further along is a tall obelisk. This was raised to the memory of [13] FRANÇOIS FOUCART (1781-1850), an Officer of the Imperial Guard of France, Chevalier of the Légion d'Honneur and Professor of Fencing at the Royal Academy in Paris. As Foucart had spent 40 years in Glasgow as a fencing teacher, his grateful students raised this imposing memorial to him in 1863 as a testament to his popularity. In passing, it is worth noting that it was a Dr Foucart of Glasgow who, on the morning of 29 June 1850, went to the assistance of the Prime Minister, Sir Robert Peel, when he was thrown from his horse while riding up Constitution Hill in London. Peel was badly injured and died on 2 July.

Continue right to the end of the *Upsilon* section, and you will find a surprise waiting for you. As the high-rise flats loom closer, you cannot fail to miss the massive two-tier mausoleum to your right, high above your head. There

lies [14] Major ARCHIBALD DOUGLAS MONTEATH (d1842). David Cousin designed this monument in the style of a Knights Templar church at a cost of £800. At certain times of the year, when the full moon shines on it, it could be mistaken for a mysterious flying saucer.

Major Monteath was an officer with the East India Company. However, the thought had crossed more than one Glasgow mind that his wealth seemed excessively out of proportion to his relatively lowly rank and profession. But a reasonably plausible explanation did eventually emerge. It was said that in India an elephant suddenly stampeded at the ceremonial procession of a certain Maharajah. Immediately the alert and intrepid Major Monteath galloped after it, away into the hinterland, and, you probably guessed – caught the rampaging animal and brought it under control. On that day the elephant's load was a casket of precious stones and jewellery. The Major rescued the casket – and then kept it as booty! Perhaps he thought it was a reasonable reward for his exertions.

GO DOWN THE PATH

GO DOWN THE STEPS

Now you have to take a complete change of direction. Arriving at the junction below Monteath's mausoleum, turn left and walk down the 17 steps. Continue along the path towards the brewery until you reach a second set of steps on your right. Go down these steps, turn right again and then go down the eight stone steps on your left.

Now head north again, up the new tarmac path, with a

retaining stone wall to your right. At the top of the rise there is some new path lighting and, just opposite the silver birch trees growing on your left (in the *Beta* section) raise your eyes above you to your right, directly below the towering Monteath monument. You see that you are now under the blackened plinth that supports the imposing statue of [15] Lieutenant-Colonel ALEXANDER HOPE PATTISON (1787-1835), a

GO UP THE TARMAC PATH

veteran of the Peninsular War, his battle honours listed on the stone. Commander-in-Chief of the Second West India

Regiment, his portrait on the sides of the plinth, is surrounded by Greek helmets and swords. His dramatic statue, erected in 1838, looks stoically westwards over the city (in spite of having lost one of his stone arms) and reveals his still commanding appearance. Pattison died at Nassau in the Bahamas and was buried there nine years before Glasgow's Necropolis was officially opened.

In complete contrast is his brother, the notorious surgeon [16] Dr GRANVILLE SHARP PATTISON (1791-1851), who also rests nearby. As a teacher in the Medical School of the High Street College in 1813, Dr Sharp was just as eager as any other medical man to increase his understanding of anatomy by dissecting recently deceased human bodies. But in December of that year, he overstepped the mark. Mrs Janet McAllaster, wife of a rich Glasgow wool merchant was hardly cold in her grave in the Ramshorn Kirkyard (which we shall later visit), when she was secretly dug up. Her body was then discovered on the dissecting table at the college. Then forensic history was evidently made in Scotland when, for the first time, a body was positively identified by teeth impressions.

Dr Pattison was brought to court, but at the end of his trial walked out again a free man; insufficient evidence was provided by the prosecution to obtain a conviction. Pattison sailed to America and, two years later, furthered his career in New York. At New York University, 'G. S. Pattison Esq., FRCS' became a respected Professor of Anatomy. After he died, his body was brought back across the Atlantic for burial. As far as we know, no one has tried to dig him up.

Continue further north along the *Beta* section, as the well gritted path slopes down. You pass the 'Bridge of Sighs' to your left, but continue walking north as the path descends. On your left, just as you reach the junction, you will see that one of the last stones is a weather-beaten and peeling square block where, at the base, you can just make out the name of Belfast-born **[17] WILLIAM THOMSON, LORD KELVIN**

(1824-1907), one of the founders of the science of physics. He added some important words to the English language – 'thermodynamics,' for example.

Thomson was barely 11 years old when he became a student at the University of Glasgow. His skill at designing scientific instruments was to lead to the laying of the first transatlantic telegraph cable in 1866. Thomson also redesigned the nautical compass and improved depth-sounding equipment. One old P&O captain called him 'the greatest friend of the sailor who ever lived'. Beside the original stone a fine new granite memorial has recently been erected by the Royal Philosophical Society of Glasgow of which Lord Kelvin was twice president.

Walk on down to where you meet the other wider path and then follow it ahead of you to the north as it takes you gently uphill, veering slightly to the right. Ahead, but on your left, at a junction where a narrower path arrives to meet the main one you are on, you cannot miss a solitary square stone plinth to a man who is not here. This is the

monument to [18] WILLIAM MILLER (d1872, aged 62), a former medical student and cabinet maker, who won immortality by writing the *Wee Willie Winkie* lullaby that, all over the world, put generations of children to sleep. Tragically, Miller died from a leg ulcer. Today, his body lies in a rubble-strewn, unmarked grave at Tollcross Cemetery in the east end of Glasgow. Some people who see this monument have said that, later, as the lights come on in Cathedral Square, they have looked back into the gloaming that bathes the Necropolis and have imagined that they see the wispy figure of Miller's Wee Willie Winkie skipping across the 'Bridge of Sighs' in his nightgown!

With this delightful image still in your imagination, take the first sharp turning to the right, up a hairpin bend climbing now towards the landmark Monteath Mausoleum high up on the main plateau of the Necropolis. Just before you reach the top of the path turn to the right down through the gravestones and then walk hard left below the main path. In front of you, facing the Cathedral, and on a lower terrace almost in line with the 'Bridge of Sighs' is the tomb of [19] JAMES DAVIDSON of Ruchill (1772-1850). It is designed in the shape of a Greek temple. Davidson, a merchant who owned an estate in Lanarkshire, chose JT

Rochead (1814-78) to design it. Along with the aforementioned Wallace Monument, Rochead's work includes the building later to become the BBC's former headquarters at Queen Margaret Drive. Rochead worked for the Davidsons in 1851, using a relatively restrained style of architecture, before he exerted all his energies into what is known as the 'Scottish baronial' style and produced the kind of castle-like buildings that usually feature in the final act of pantomimes.

Return to the path and then walk across it to an opening on the left. Walk north for about 403 paces along a narrow terrace, with a retaining wall to your right. You will already glimpse a foreboding and dramatic façade that looks directly onto the Cathedral, the [20] AITKENS of DALMOAK mausoleum, designed by James Hamilton and built in 1875. It is the largest burial monument in the Necropolis. Today, spreading its wings, a headless angel faces westwards, framed on each side by mighty iron-grilled gates and massive Ionic pillars. The sepulchre below is divided into four vaults, for different members of the family.

Return again to the main path and finish the short climb to the plateau above. Lowering over you as you reach the brow of the hill is the forbidding 35-foot high monument to [21] WILLIAM McGAVIN (1773-1832), with its statue of the deceased by sculptor Robert Forrest, pointing to a book in its hand. McGavin was born in Ayrshire where he worked as a weaver, but then turned to teaching and finally became a bank manager and preacher. McGavin (known popularly as 'The Protestant' – after the anti-Catholic periodical he published) worked tirelessly to discredit the Roman Catholic Church, but he came off worst in the end when the latter successfully sued him for libel.

Now turn to your right and go to the third stone at the edge of the path. Facing you (in the *Sigma* section), is a stone that proudly carries the Polish Eagle. Here you will find [22] Lieutenant JOSEPH GOMOSZYNSKI (d1845, aged 32), a soldier in the Polish Army. After Napoleon's downfall, because the Poles had been Napoleon's allies, the Congress of Vienna (1815) assigned half of Poland to Russia. The remainder of Poland was to be granted self-government, but the Russians denied this to the Poles and so severely oppressed them that in 1830, with a great uprising, the Polish people tried to regain their freedom. Ruthlessly, the Russians crushed them. Many of Poland's fighting men, like Gomoszynski, had to escape into exile. He died at Greenock.

Two graves immediately to his right (in lair No 54, still in the *Sigma* section and also at the edge of the path) is the grave of the campaigning journalist [23] PETER MACKENZIE (1799-1875). In 1847, when starvation and typhus trailed death through the poorest parts of Glasgow, Mackenzie organised soup kitchens and, in that ghastly year, he uncovered a callous fraud that involved

PETER MACKENZIE

the deliberate adulteration of ground oats (known as meal) destined for human consumption. A Highland Relief Committee had been formed in the city to dispatch cargoes of meal to help Highland areas suffering famine. Alexander Bannatyne, a grain merchant in Hope Street, was given an £11,000 contract to supply and deliver the meal. However, Mackenzie's friend, Alex Lauder, got wind that Mr Bannatyne was adulterating the meal with 'bran, thirds and sawdust'!

As soon as the news reached him, Peter decided that he and Alex would, that very midnight, slip into the place where Bannatyne's men were bagging the meal for shipment – the basement of the Unitarian Chapel in Union Street. There they secretly managed to remove samples of the meal that were to prove the charge of adulteration indisputably.

Bannatyne was sentenced to four months in jail and fined £400. Then to Mackenzie's dismay, the culprit was mysteriously released without a fine, and was even paid for the meal. Is it possible that he had friends in high places?

Go now behind the Mackenzie grave towards the 40-feet high monument shaped like a Moon rocket with a domed top, believed to be made of Irish granite. Standing in the *Sigma* section, it covers the last resting place of [24] WILLIAM DUNN of Duntocher (1770-1849). It was said of Willie Dunn (an engineer and entrepreneur in the cotton industry) that he was so mean that, had he been a ghost, he would not have given you a fright without demanding payment. He was a highly successful industrialist but he had a strange hobby – he took out writs against people, but mostly against his neighbour, Lord Blantyre. The disputes were usually about estate boundaries.

In this regard, he was, oddly enough, always most generous to his lawyers whom he kept regularly in business.

On his sick bed, he told a visiting minister that he had overcome his greatest enemy. The minister offered up a prayer in thanksgiving, thinking that Willie meant that his greatest enemy was Sin. Imagine the good man's shock to learn that Willie had been referring to Lord Blantyre!

Once, when Willie donated only a miserly two guineas to a charity, a friend said to him, 'How mean! You can't take your money to Heaven!' Willie replied, 'I know that perfectly well — it's the only thing I'm vexed aboot!'

Now turn left towards the north and walk on upwards, past the back of McGavin's monument, through the *Sigma* section and in the direction of the Knox pillar. You pass close to the slender obelisk in memory of a minister's daughter, [25] ELIZA JANE AIKMAN (1852-1929), its inscription facing the John Knox monument.Eliza Jane was one of those special people who, with their quiet persistence, manage radically to improve the condition of the human race. Eliza founded the Glasgow Infant Health Visitors Association. Indeed, her work established the basis for

subsequent child welfare practice in the city. Few could have guessed that the quiet girl sitting on Sundays at Anderston United Presbyterian Church, would one day make history.

Turn left now, once more, again towards the Cathedral. Walk off the grass onto the path again. On the edge of the plateau the [26] Revd RALPH WARDLAW (1779-1853) has his resting place. Wardlaw, whose white marble bust gazes serenely at your left, was a charismatic personality and his preaching was described as 'magnetic'. The good, the bad, the ugly, the beautiful, the rich and the powerful flocked to hear his fabulous phrases in his West George Street church. Unhappily, not long after Wardlaw's death, his kirk was sold to the Edinburgh and Glasgow Railway Company and used as offices for Queen Street Station.

Walk forward up the path again, towards the statue of John Knox. Notice the impressive pink Peterhead granite monument to the memory of [27] HENRY MONTEITH (1765-1848) of Carstairs. Monteith was the go-getting father-in-law of John George Hamilton (whose grave we noted in the Cathedral old churchyard). This entrepreneur owed a large part of his business success to the genius of Peter Papillon, a French chemist who left France in 1783.

In possession of a secret method for making and dyeing the highly popular Turkey-red colour onto cotton, Papillon came to Glasgow. He set himself up in business and became reasonably wealthy. Henry Monteith, meanwhile, also used the Papillon process in the production of his world-famous Glasgow bandanas. These were known locally as 'carters' hankies'. Alas, the Frenchman made the mistake of giving his business over to his sons, who virtually ruined it and

the great chemist, living in near poverty, died in his 60s around the year 1810. Monteith, however, was twice elected Lord Provost of Glasgow (1814-16 and 1818-20) and also served as the MP for Lanark Burghs.

Turn hard right now from Henry Monteith's burial place and (with John Knox high above on the left) applaud the outrageously theatrical monument on your left to [28] JOHN HENRY ALEXANDER (1807-51), the most spectacular actor-manager Glasgow has ever known. His memorial is shaped

like the stage of a Victorian theatre, with the final curtain about to fall. There is a verse tribute on the monument revealing that Alexander was a man of many parts, but the ones he played best were those of husband and father. Alexander tried to take over the old Caledonian Theatre in Dunlop Street in 1825, but Frank Seymour of the Queen Street Theatre dived in too. Alexander got the basement but Frank got the theatre proper.

While Shakespeare's 'The Scottish Play' (*Macbeth*) was playing in the basement, *The Battle of the Inch* was thundering in the theatre upstairs. Imagine the clash of sound effects and the vocal contrasts! Frank's patrons sometimes even lifted the floorboards and poured water down on John Henry's customers! Alexander eventually took over the whole building and renamed it the Theatre Royal.

Tragedy struck in February 1849 when a false fire alarm caused a panic stampede, and 65 people, desperate to escape, were crushed to death. John Henry never really recovered from the shock of that terrible night. He died not long afterwards, a broken man. His lasting legacy was his invention, the 'Great Gun Trick', whereby brave souls

caught bullets in their teeth much to the amazement of audiences all over the world.

Two graves down to the right from John Henry's stone, is the massive white bust of [29] DUGALD MOORE (1805-41), a Glasgow poet born in Stockwell Street. As a boy Dugald was indentured to a comb maker, but his master was almost driven insane because his young apprentice was too poor-sighted to touch a comb without breaking its teeth! The craftsman begged Dugald's mother to take him off to some other occupation in which weak eyesight would be less of a problem.

One of Dugald's poems ('To the Vitrified Fort in Glen Nevis') is like a scene from one of the works of Sir Edwin Landseer (1802-73), the artist who painted 'The Monarch of the Glen':

The rising beams of hope may come and gather
O'er other lands — they will not visit us.
The dark stone looking through the silent heather,
The fort — exclaims, it was not always thus.

From Moore's grave, turn north and walk straight up all the way to the Knox monument. To your left looms an enormous blackened stone tower, marking the grave of the [30] Revd DUNCAN MACFARLAN (1771-1857). MacFarlan was minister of Drymen Church after his father (1792), then Principal of Glasgow University (1823) and finally minister of Glasgow Cathedral (1824). He was also Moderator of the General Assembly of the Church of Scotland twice (1819 & 1842).

You will then see, right below Knox, the large granite casket raised to the

memory of [31] JAMES EWING (1774-1853), the same James Ewing who persuaded the Merchants of Glasgow to support the creation of the Necropolis. James Ewing was twice Dean of Guild for the city. He was also Lord Provost, and a Member of Parliament for Glasgow (1833-4), after the passing of the Reform Bill.

For a fee of £5,000 James Ewing bought a mansion at the head of Queen Street, with its adjacent land. A few years later, he sold it all to the Edinburgh & Glasgow Railway Company at a price of one guinea per square yard. Part of the price was paid in railway shares. A nice little earner!

Ewing's house was surrounded by fine trees which provided accommodation for flocks of crows. They earned Mr Ewing the nickname of 'Craw Jamie'. However, Jamie did not hoard his wealth and Glasgow has reason to be eternally grateful for his generosity to the people and the City of Glasgow.

From the Ewing grave turn east and take around 60 paces forward, crossing the path. Behind the first row of gravestones is the granite block marking the presence of [32] Sir JAMES LUMSDEN (1808-79), Lord Provost of the city in 1866. His father (also James Lumsden) was Treasurer of Glasgow Royal Infirmary, and it is said that his expertise at fundraising was of the most efficient 'getting blood out of a stone' variety (his statue can still be seen in the Cathedral precinct beside the Infirmary). James Lumsden Snr founded the Clydesdale Bank in 1837 and became Lord Provost in 1843.

Turn right now and walk north until you reach the main path. On your right, the large polished granite tomb at the end of the row (shaped rather like a comfortable pink sofa) is that of [33] ROBERT BAIRD of Auchmeddon (d1856, aged 50). In the 1830s, the exploration of 'blackband' ironstone in Lanarkshire made that base metal as good as gold. Robert Baird was one of eight brothers brought up on

a farm near Airdrie. The family had the capital to found the Gartsherrie Ironworks and had become, by mid-century, the largest producers of pig iron in Scotland. Robert also served as Dean of Guild of Glasgow (1854-6).

Long after Robert was gone, his brother James gave a hint of how rich the Bairds had become. In 1873 he gave £500,000 to promote the teaching of the Gospel – an astronomical sum in those days!

RANDOLPH AND ELDER WORKS (1969), COURTESY OF RCAHMS

On the path, turn right again and head east along the path for 60 paces to the end of the next row of graves (still in the *Epsilon* section). There is a stone here over the grave of [34] JOHN ELDER (1824-69). The Elders were a great shipbuilding family, but son John had star quality. He was born just 13 years after Henry Bell persuaded the Wood brothers to build his paddle steamer, the *Comet*. Shipbuilding skills ran deep in his blood and John grew up to be pioneer shipbuilder Robert Napier's right-hand man.

Elder's greatest talent was his ingenuity in designing marine engines. He created a combination high-pressure and low-pressure engine which saved 30 to 40 per cent in coal consumption but shipowners did not believe him! Only after much coaxing did they buy the engine. John Elder's name is not only remembered here, but also in the pleasant Elder Park that Govan folk wander through. A statue of his wife stands there, and the Elder Cottage Hospital was situated not far from the park.

From the Elder memorial you now need to walk south towards the hills on the horizon, the two large brewery chimneys and the wide path that runs beside the boundary wall above the old Ladywell Quarry. Here you can see a wonderful panorama of the city spread out in front of you. Turn hard left (following the path eastwards) and go past five ranks of stones until you reach a set of low semi-circular steps at the end.

Here lie the [35] **PROFESSORS** of Glasgow University. When their time in this vale of tears was ended, the Dons of the University and their families were buried at Blackfriars Churchyard,  close to the old College in the High Street. They were then all moved here in 1876 when the graveyard made way for the College Goods Station. Railways had precedence.

Continue walking east again until you reach the last row of stones and turn sharp left. Still in the *Epsilon* section, a few metres ahead, you will see a large white granite memorial, a reminder to the people of Glasgow of the ultimate price paid by its dedicated firemen on the night of 28 March 1960, when the sky over the city glowed red and orange at Cheapside Street, Anderston.

THE CHEAPSIDE STREET FIRE (1960), COURTESY OF STRATHCLYDE FIRE & RESCUE

Later that evening, news spread that 14 men of the [36] **GLASGOW FIRE BRIGADE SERVICE** and five of the **SALVAGE CORPS** had died, when the blazing whisky bond they were hosing down suddenly exploded around them. Also here remembered are

the seven heroic firefighters who died at the Kilbirnie Street fire on 25 August 1972.

Leaving the Fire Service memorial stone, walk north. When you reach the path turn left across it, heading diagonally north-west about 110 paces over the open field, past the row of trees (on your right) and in the direction of the tall industrial chimney visible over the horizon.

Stop in the middle of the row of memorial stones which face you (in the *Zeta* section), in front of the pink pedimented tomb of [37] Sir HUGH REID (d1935, aged 75). A locomotive builder, Reid was in charge of the Hydepark Works in the heyday of the North British Locomotive Company. Even when he died, the company was still sending locomotives down Springburn Road to the docks, from where they were shipped off to faraway places with exotic names. Early on Sunday mornings people would line the streets to wave goodbye to those giant engines.

Walk to the far end of the row of gravestones which runs westwards directly behind Sir Hugh Reid. Then turn left, passing the two muscular bronze angels (green with patina) guarding the granite temple dedicated to [38] ALEXANDER ALLAN (1780-1854), a Temperance campaigner and director of the Allan Line, a transatlantic shipping company.

Just further on, at the end of the next row (facing south) and to your left (in lair No 103), is the pink granite obelisk of a blind minister, the **[39] Revd GEORGE MATHESON** (1842-1906). Born in Edinburgh, Matheson ministered in Innellan, and wrote the world-famous hymn, 'O Love that wilt not let me go'. It is said that Matheson wrote the third line of his verse as 'I climb the rainbow through the rain', but the then organist of Glasgow Cathedral, Dr Albert Pearce, who was

putting the music to George's words, changed the word 'climb' to 'trace', so that the words and music flowed more smoothly. It seems that George was not best pleased, but after a while he did agree that the word had to be 'trace'.

Walk on in the *Zeta* section towards the John Knox statue. Immediately on your right is a large grey granite tomb with a curved semi-circular top. In the middle of the memorial is the green bronze head of **[40] WALTER MacFARLANE** (d1885, aged 69). Walter used iron as an art medium.

MacFarlane's business began in a small foundry in 1850 near the Saracen Head Inn along the Gallowgate, but moved first to Anderston, and then to Possilpark, because

MACFARLANE'S SHOWROOM, COURTESY OF THE RCAHMS

of the repeated expansion of his trade. His fine architectural ironwork can still be seen all over the world today. He produced the frame for Gardner's warehouse, the iron building still seen in Jamaica Street. His iron lattice designs in the Durbar Hall of the Maharajah of Mysore are among the finest examples of the art. His craftsmen were able to mould iron as easily as we now mould plastic.

Opposite MacFarlane's tomb is that of the German engineer, [41] HENRY DUBS (d1876, aged 60). In earlier and better times his portrait bust sheltered under the stone canopy. Dubs founded the Glasgow Steam Locomotive Works at Polmadie in 1863. In the great 'Age of the Railway', Glasgow abounded with railway engine companies – Neilson & Company, the Clyde Locomotive Works, the Atlas Works and, of course, the North British Locomotive Company (first at Hydepark Street, Anderston, and ultimately in Springburn where the works retained the old name, Hydepark). Amalgamations took place until the North British Locomotive Company made Springburn the locomotive-building capital of Europe. The skills and experience of Henry Dubs ensured that the Glasgow products were given due recognition as being of the highest quality.

Walk forwards towards John Knox again. On your right you pass the dark and enigmatic mausoleum of [42] JOHN HOULDSWORTH (1807-59) and family. Houldsworth was a senior Bailie of the City of Glasgow who established the Anderston Foundry Company. Outside, the tomb is guarded by white marble figures of Hope and Charity (Faith stands inside). Further on towards the Knox monument, in the *Omega* section, you cannot fail to spot the figure of [43]

CHARLES TENNANT of Rollox (1768-1838), sitting slumped rather dejectedly, high on top of his tomb. Originally trained as a weaver, Tennant was 31 when he first successfully achieved the manufacture of bleaching powder at his St Rollox chemical works.

He was sharply aware of the atmospheric pollution his works were creating and so he ordered the building of the world's highest chimney – 450 feet high – in an attempt to dissipate the fumes into the upper atmosphere – 'Tennant's Stalk' was a Glasgow landmark well into the 20th century.

ST ROLLOX CHEMICAL WORKS (1964), COURTESY OF THE RCAHMS

Over the decades, however, the St Rollox Works has been one of the city's worst eyesores. Chemical waste was dumped in the Sighthill area, so causing a deadly spread that local people nicknamed the 'Stinking Ocean'. In spite of his work with dangerous chemicals, Charles Tennant lived to the ripe old age of 70.

Turn north once more, facing the exquisite octagonal Moorish kiosk (tower) dedicated to [44] Dr WILLIAM RAE WILSON (1772-1849), a Paisley solicitor who was devastated by the death of his young wife only 18 months after they had married. To restore some meaning to his life again, he travelled extensively, exploring in particular the Middle East. His book, *Travels in Egypt and the Holy Land* (1823), tells his story.

Dr Wilson died in London and was brought to Glasgow for burial. The design of his tomb by the architect JA Bell would not look out of place in Palestine. Apparently no wood, iron or lead was used in its construction.

Now the time has come to begin the descent from the summit of the Necropolis. Go past the left (west) of Dr Wilson's monument, walking down the grassy path, with the wooden fencing on your left. Make for the concrete steps and their iron handrails which you will see through the trees. Be careful as this route may be slippery.

Just before you reach the steps you will see a monument immediately below you on the left, a heavy pillar with an urn on top. Here lies the [45] Revd ALEXANDER OGILVIE BEATTIE DD (1785-1858). He was minister of the Gordon Street United Presbyterian Church and would have been minister of St Vincent Street United Presbyterian Church, had he lived. The latter is still in existence, designed by 'Greek' Thomson and it was appropriate that Thomson also designed this monument to Beattie. The stone itself was sculpted by John Mossman, patriarch of the famous Glasgow sculptors who carved the majority of the headstones at the Necropolis.

Not far below the Revd Beattie is the memorial to [46] HUGH COGAN (d1855, aged 63). It is likely that Rochead designed Cogan's monument. It stands further round the curve of the path from the Black mausoleum and on the opposite side of Willie Motherwell. Do have a look at it. Its severe straight lines have a forbidding appearance – four square columns with a plain canopy and a solid base. No fancy urns or faces or convolutions here. Rochead had not yet gone wildly Scottish baronial! Being an elder in the Free Kirk, and founding the first Glasgow Building Society, were among Hugh Cogan's lifetime achievements.

Next, go down onto the path and turn up left into the curving top end of the *Gamma* section. There, to your right, is the small temple dedicated to **[47] WILLIAM MOTHERWELL** (1797-1835), a Glasgow poet, born in the High Street. Willie Motherwell's poetry often had a Nordic theme, and some of the heroic characters of his verse are carved here. A fit of apoplexy killed the poet in 1835, and so his transmission to the Necropolis was sudden. For the next 16 years, an old friend came occasionally to pin a snatch of Willie's verse at the graveside. This drew attention to the lack of a suitable monument to the poet and eventually public subscription provided the funds for sculptor James Fillans to create this monument in 1851. When Willie's head wasn't up in the clouds above an imaginary Parnassus, he was Sheriff Clerk Depute for Renfrew and the editor of the *Glasgow Courier*.

It is likely that the very first elaborate mausoleum at the Necropolis was commissioned by Robert Black in 1837. You can see it now on your left, set into the hillside, a Greek temple with rusty iron gates. It was built for the interment of Black's daughter, **[48] CATHERINE BLACK**, who was just 12 years old when she

CATHERINE BLACK

died in 1837. Inside, the dates inscribed reveal that five of this unfortunate man's children died before they reached the age of 21.

Walk down again onto the main path. Turn left and go down (westwards) across the grass and meet another set of concrete steps with handrails: walk down seven separate sets of steps to the roadway below and then turn right along it. Then walk north for about 40 paces. Three rows of graves to the right above you, behind a large tree, you will see the grave of a much respected woman – **[49] CORLINDA LEE** (d1900), Queen of the Gypsies and a real Queen in the eyes of many others. Glasgow has always loved fairgrounds–although they were never called that in Glasgow – they

were known as 'the shows' or 'carnival' – where the chair o' planes, the cake-walk and the habby-horses brought thrills and spills into the depressing life of the city. Here, the gypsies, the 'travelling folk', were always welcome. The monument once displayed Corlinda's regal likeness, but vandalism has struck since she was laid here.

If continuing down the steep steps may be hazardous because of the weather conditions, an alternative is to turn back the way you came, walking towards the 'Bridge of Sighs.' You eventually pass the solitary stone of Willie Miller

ABSALOM'S PILLAR

again. Forty paces further on, take a sharp right turn along the terrace, going north with the black iron railings to your left and you will come to **[50]** the **JEWISH CEMETERY.** (www.sjac.org.uk) The mighty pillar in front of you is a copy of Absalom's Column in the Valley of the Kings, Jerusalem. Joseph Levi, who was mentioned earlier, was the first arrival here in 1832. By 1857 the Enclosure was closed because there was no more space available – Jewish people are buried with no more than one body to each grave.

Sadly, your visit to the Necropolis is now concluded. Go back to the head of the 'Bridge of Sighs', cross it and exit by the main gates.

St David's Burying Ground

(Ramshorn Kirk), 98 Ingram Street,
GLASGOW G1 1ES

The original Ramshorn Church was built in 1720 in what was then Canon Street. It had a small graveyard around it, and its lairs were sold to defray the cost of building the kirk. The new burying ground to the east and north of the kirk was created in 1780 by the Town Council. Then Canon Street was widened to become Ingram Street, and at the street frontage of the graveyard some lairs were lost. Designed by the architect Thomas Rickman of Birmingham, St David's (*Ramshorn Kirk*) of 1824 was the elegant replacement for an old, staid place of worship.

In those days Glasgow had a Town Superintendent of Public Works, the lawyer Dr James Cleland, who decided that he could best do his job by running the city all by himself! Indeed, he took away Rickman's drawings for the new building to a secret retreat, cut himself off from the world for three days and then came back with his own modifications. He had added a crypt and steps to the front door — which folk later said threatened life and limb!

That crypt, which became his final resting-place, is still there. And above it, the ornate architecture has a tower designed to provide a 'ring of bells'. Alas, not one sublime tinkle has ever issued from that tower! Books, however, poured from the pen of Dr Cleland, a most prolific writer — *The Annals of Glasgow* (1816) and *An historical account of the bills of mortality and the probability of human life, in Glasgow and other large towns* (1836). Hardly bedtime reading.

When you first arrive (and before you enter the grounds of the church), don't forget to look at the street just out from the gate into the new burying ground. Stand facing the church: to the right of the building, faintly grooved into the

concrete pavement is a thin cross. Above one side of the crosspiece are the initials 'A. F.' and on the other side, 'R. E.'. Fortunately, the bones of the printers [1] ROBERT (1707-76) and ANDREW (1712-75) FOULIS were not disturbed when the street was widened. Passers-by have been walking over them for over 200 years.

The Foulis brothers were 18th-century printers who produced books that matched the best in Europe. They worked mostly for Glasgow University and their volumes in Latin and Greek are quite superb. Copies are still found throughout Europe; four are kept in the King's Library of the British Museum. Robert Foulis founded an Academy of

Arts in Glasgow, but (strangely) received little public support. This venture finally drained him of all his funds. After Andrew died his remaining assets were sold off in London for a pittance.

Most of the stones in the old burying ground (that is the part immediately around the kirk) have been harshly bruised by time and tempest. Now walk along the pavement past the front of the church to the left-hand side. Enter the gate. Immediately to the west (to your left), set into the wall of the neighbouring Strathclyde University building, is the stone of the [2] GLASSFORD family. JOHN GLASSFORD of Dougalston (1715-83) was one of the four young men to

whom Provost Andrew Cochrane attributed Glasgow's development as a world-famous centre of commerce. The others were Spiers, Cunningham and Ritchie. They were some of the famous 'Tobacco Lords'.

John Glassford was a flamboyant, ambitious man who became breathtakingly rich. But, while, with the onset of the American War of Independence, many of his contemporaries lost their fortunes, John did not wait that long to lose his. For he gambled like mad. He would bet on beetles climbing a wall and only rarely picked a winning one! He even built an outhouse on his estate just for gambling and games of chance. While his colleagues supported Britain in the War of Independence, Glassford, just to be awkward, supported the American revolutionaries. So he died a ruined and unpopular man.

Nevertheless, he owned Shawfield Mansion situated close to the street named after him – Glassford Street. In December 1745 Bonnie Prince Charlie lodged there, during his uneasy visit to the city. There, Charlie met the ill-starred Clementina Walkinshaw, the woman whom he treated so cruelly – a sorry tale but one beyond the bounds of this book.

Return the way you came and enter the grounds of the

church by the gate on the right. Walk to the back of the church, where it is shaded by trees. You can still see the old wall, now incorporated into an extension block. Somewhere in the foundations is the grave of [3] ROBERT (*Robin*) CARRICK (d1821, aged 84), a likely son of the manse. Whatever diet he consumed as a minister's son, the part he seems to have shunned was the milk of human kindness. Robin had not one drop of it. He was the meanest man of his day.

Hence, he was just the manager for the old Ship Bank! He detested having to hand money over his counter. His housekeeper and niece, Miss Paisley, was even meaner. She would haggle for an hour with the butcher to wheedle a farthing off the price of beef. This miserly manager wouldn't even help members of his own family who were in financial distress. One day, however, he got his come-uppance.

Warehouseman John McIlquham, who kept his considerable funds in the Ship Bank, was progressively so disgusted by Robin Carrick's niggardly contributions to charity that, one morning, he sent a servant round to the bank with a cheque to withdraw £10,000! Banker Carrick's legs gave way under him! He recovered sufficiently to send the servant back to his master, saying, 'He must be ill! Get a doctor for Mr McIlquham!' The servant took the cheque back and reported Robin's comments.

John McIlquham was livid. He rushed round to the Ship Bank and roared at the banker that he wanted a £50 donation from Carrick to a well-known local charity immediately – or he would withdraw all his money! Carrick made a hasty donation, and, smiling, John McIlquham tore up his £10,000 cheque.

To be fair, while banks were collapsing all over Glasgow, Robin Carrick made sure that his clients suffered no loss. By the time he died he had become a millionaire.

Walk north across the grass and between the central burial enclosure – known as *Paradise*, as only the well-to-do could be buried there. At the first corner of the enclosure that you come to is the large flat stone set into the grass that tells the story of tragic [4] DAVID McQUATER (d1780, aged 15), an apprentice brick-layer who fell to his death from a scaffold. He was just 15 years and three months old. McQuater's mourners were at pains to record on this stone that David was a very fine and promising young man.

Go on along the wall of the enclosure. Only a few steps away members of the [5] MONTEITH family are interred here under an imposing stone, boldly carved (and formerly railed off) with the heading that it is 'Sacred to the Memory of HENRY MONTEITH of Carstairs' (1765-1848). His wife

Christina is buried here, along with a number of her children. She had 14 children in all but only five were alive when she died. The stone was erected by her youngest child, Robert Monteith.

Carry on round the remains of a rusty *mortsafe* and you will see an empty space on the wall where a plaque has been gouged out. A stone on the outer face of the west inner partition wall, near the south end, marks where [6] WILLIAM FRIEND DURANT (d1821, aged 19) was buried. Durant, a multi-talented student at Glasgow University, was born in Dorset, but came to Scotland for his higher education. A good-hearted lad, he made a host of friends in the city but illness cut him down while he was still a teenager. Hundreds of fellow students and friends mourned at his grave on that fateful November day.

A MORTSAFE

In the north-west corner of the burial ground, framed by tall buildings, you will find the [7] Revd JAMES FISHER (d1775, aged 78), his stone propped up at an angle to make it easier to read. He was the first minister of the Associated Congregation of Shuttle Street. They were an intense group and not too happily disposed towards certain Episcopalians who had decided to build themselves a church in 1750 down by Glasgow Green.

Andrew Hunter, a master mason who was a member of the Shuttle Street congregation, won the contract to build the 'Piskie' (Episcopal) church, but this displeased his fellow members. They knew, of course, that the Devil would be helping to build this church beside the Green and told Andrew he must refuse to accept the contract. He replied with a remark similar to, 'Awa an' chase yoursels!' – and was promptly excommunicated! Indeed, an old woman claimed to have seen the Devil in the 'Piskie' building early one morning – obviously working on the nightshift. The Shuttle Street church has long since vanished, but St Andrew's-by-the-Green still flourishes, not as a church, but as a suite of offices.

Walk into the north (top) end of the burial enclosure (*Paradise*). Go along the inside face of the east inner partition wall. It forms a kind of closed rectangle with the west inner partition wall. About halfway along the east wall, you will find [8] ALEXANDER GLEN. There is no particular reason to remember him, but his son, William Glen, has a claim to a fragment of immortality. Many writers of Glasgow

history have assumed that the son lies with the father. He doesn't. Willie Glen was a poet but an impoverished one — poverty being a hazard of that trade. His heyday was the second decade of the 19th century. When Wellington defeated the French at Vitoria, Spain, in June 1813, the conflict inspired his poem, 'The Battle of Vitoria'! Here's a snatch of it:

> The English Rose was ne'er sae red,
> The Shamrock waved where glory led,
> And the Scottish Thistle raised its head,
> An' smiled upon Vitoria.
> Loud was the battle's stormy swell,
> Whare thousands fought and mony fell;
> But the Glasgow heroes bore the bell
> At the battle of Vitoria.

But probably Glen's most famous effusion was his Jacobite song, 'Wae's me for Prince Cherlie'. Peter Mackenzie, that most daring investigative journalist of the 19th century, reveals in his book *Old Reminiscences of Glasgow and the West of Scotland* (1890) that, when Willie Glen died, his rich relatives refused to allow him burial in the family lair at the Ramshorn. Instead he was consigned to oblivion in an unmarked grave in an odd corner of the Cathedral graveyard.

Leave the enclosure by its south entrance and then go left round the end of its outside wall. Now, remember William Minnoch in the Necropolis — the man whose girlfriend was tried for murdering another lover? Well, let's find out more. Just before another mortsafe you will see a stone set into the wall. It marks the last resting place of **[9]** the FLEMING family. What the stone doesn't say is that one of the occupants

of this lair (No 5) who has claimed most attention doesn't actually have his name on the stone. He was a clerk from the Channel Islands called [10] PIERRE ÉMILE L'ANGELIER (d1857).

Fate nudged Pierre into meeting the daughter of the famous Glasgow architect James Smith, who lived in Blythswood Square. A fatal attraction flashed between them and Madeleine began a relationship with him. Her letters to him were passionate and full of promise! But she knew that marriage between a girl of her rank and station and a poor clerk was out of the question. Minnoch, older than her but of good stock, was her official 'intended' and would keep her in the manner to which she was accustomed.

Eventually she tired of Pierre and wanted to end the affair. But he threatened to show her letters to her father and, afraid of the scandal, Madeleine allowed their clandestine meetings to continue, with Pierre slipping into her home without her family knowing. Madeleine often treated Pierre to a cup or two of cocoa made with her own fair hands. Simultaneously, Pierre began to suffer spells of grogginess. He died in March 1857 with enough arsenic in his body to kill two dozen people.

Now it came to light that Madeleine had been buying arsenic for her complexion – or so she said. The obvious suspect, Madeleine was tried for the murder of L'Angelier, but walked from court on a *Not Proven* verdict. But the scandal was rife. Her father gave up his business and the family fled forever from the city. William Minnoch jilted Madeleine, and she too left the city for London, where her sparkling personality had once made her a popular hostess. She claimed that at one of her soirées she served a cup of cocoa to George Bernard Shaw! Later she married and had children but then separated and moved to New York where she died in 1928 in her nineties, known as Lena Wardle Sheehy.

Across the path on the east wall of the graveyard, facing the Fleming plot, is the stone of [11] the PROVAND family, among whom was ANDREW DRYBURGH PROVAND (1838-

1915), the Liberal MP for the Blackfriars Division of Glasgow. But, another Provand, George, was a house painter in the early 1800s. He bought the house of the man reputed to be the richest

timber merchant in the city. He was certainly the most ugly. Bob Dreghorn, 'Dragon' as he was called, had a face that turned milk sour! He had the unnerving habit of following young ladies along Argyle Street without actually speaking to them.

Dreghorn ended up a recluse. His mansion in Clyde Street was close to where the St Andrew's Roman Catholic Cathedral now stands. Dreghorn committed suicide in his own home and his ghost was said to haunt the place thereafter.

In the 1820s, when 'bodysnatching' was at its height, some daft people looked in at the window of George Provand's paint store, which was just by his house, and saw red splashes on the floor and immediately decided George was a body snatcher, although it was not gore on the floor of the store – only red paint! They set about wrecking the big house while, out of the back door, George sprinted away for his life. Richard Campbell, the ringleader of the wreckers, was brought to court and granted the dubious honour of being the last man to be publicly scourged through the city

streets. After that, he and three of his cronies were sentenced to be transported abroad for 14 years.

A sort distance along the same wall and nearer the street, a stone set into the wall proclaims the presence of the earthly remains of [12] DAVID DALE (1739-1806), a true gentleman whose trade was in cotton. David Dale was built like a Toby jug. Once, he told a friend, he had slipped on an icy pavement and had fallen all his length. His friend replied, 'Be thankful, sir, you didn't fall all your breadth!' Dale went into the trade of cotton spinning and had mills at Blantyre and Lanark. Indeed in 1786 he took Richard Arkwright, the inventor of the Water-Frame, to see a part of the River Clyde below Lanark. This led to the opening of huge spinning mills at the model industrial village of New Lanark.

Here he established a benign form of employment which incorporated education and welfare for his workers and although the idea of this great social experiment was Dale's, his son-in-law, Robert Owen, is usually given credit for this Utopian undertaking. David Dale

CARICATURE OF
DAVID DALE

left the Church of Scotland and formed his own congregation in a church built by his friend, the candlemaker Archie Paterson. They became the 'Old Scotch Independents'. Dale was their pastor for 37 years. For obvious reasons, that church was known as the 'Caun'le Kirk'. In spite of being grossly overweight, David Dale, Glasgow's favourite philanthropist, managed to reach the age of 66 before he died in 1806.

Somewhere in an unmarked plot around here, the Revd JOHN AITKEN was given burial space. He lodged in the Little Dovehill off Gallowgate in the 1820s. John did not have a church because he did not have a divinity degree, nor had he ever even been ordained. His 'cathedral' was the open space of Glasgow Green, where he addressed fairly large gatherings with his thundering eloquence. And what good advice he offered. He would tell his listeners, 'You have three companions you must keep on good terms with: firstly, your stomach, secondly, your wife and thirdly, your conscience.' He also beseeched them not to be snared by bold John Barleycorn. It was a pity that John himself yielded to temptation, joining a Glasgow group called the Cauld Whisky Drinkeronians! These men all took a solemn vow never to let water pass their lips. Alas!

One last word about John Aitken. He was often afflicted by bad toothache and, especially on cold, frosty days, he protected his cheeks, (*chafts*, as he called them), with a piece of flannel or an old worsted stocking filled with warm salt.

You can leave the new burying ground now, to seek the deeper gloom of the Crypt.

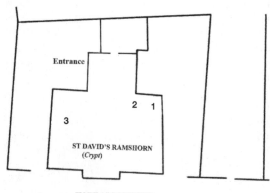

Entrance

2 1

3

ST DAVID'S RAMSHORN
(Crypt)

INGRAM STREET

St David's Crypt

(Ramshorn Kirk)

The crypt is not currently open to the general public, as it is in an unrestored state and is used as a scenery and theatrical properties store. Entry to it is via the office/stage door entrance, and is at the discretion of the University of Strathclyde's Director of Drama or the Theatre Administrator, who (on behalf of the University of Strathclyde) manages the Ramshorn Theatre now located in the former church on the floor above. However, if you are fortunate enough to gain entry, you will see that, in this dim and dusty chamber, even Dracula wouldn't feel at home. It is partly above ground level.

Right in the north-east corner of the crypt, a wall plaque does nothing to increase the joy of the visit. The inscription records the spot as the resting place of one [1] JAMES DARNLEY, but that is all that is legible. Was it, though, a shiver of black humour which inspired the sculptor to shape this plaque into a coffin?

Immediately next to the coffin shape, the sadness of

Glasgow man [2] ALEX BROOM is recorded forever on his stone plaque. Tragedy stalked his family in the autumn of 1827. His daughter, Janet, ten months old, died on 29 September and his wife, Mary Rennie, followed Janet to the crypt five days later. His agony seems frozen into this dismal place.

Over in the middle of the western wall you will find a graceful tribute to [3] Dr JAMES CLELAND on a large, decorated panel, recording the gratitude of Glasgow Corporation. Cleland was a builder who helped to  surround Glasgow Cross with tenements and shops. But he supervised the building of St George's Church and supplied the design for the new High School of Glasgow without accepting a penny in payment. No wonder the Council appointed him Superintendent of Statute Labour – a post he held for 27 years.

There was no end to the work Dr Cleland did for his city. In the hard times of 1819-20, with admirable single-mindedness, he made improvements at Glasgow Green, providing work for unemployed weavers. He introduced cattle markets to the city, also standardising weights and measures used by city traders.

At his retirement in 1834, the city had a 'whip-round' for him. £4,500 was raised. He kept on writing into his 70th year and it was in 1840 that they laid him to rest in the crypt he had designed.

But, enough is enough! It's time to get out of here ... lingering too long in this place could cause frostbite of the soul!

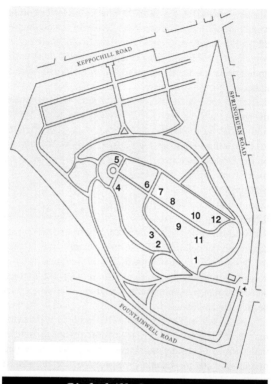

Sighthill Cemetery

300 Springburn Road,
GLASGOW G21 1SE

L ike many famous cities, the City of Glasgow is built on a series of hills. To reach its northern suburbs, you have to cross the M8 from the city centre and make your way into Springburn and the surrounding areas. But the journey, by car or public transport, does not take long and although Springburn is certainly higher than the city centre, within its boundaries Sighthill Cemetery (1840) is even higher.

The beautifully groomed entrance on Springburn Road, with imposing gates and a very Egyptian-looking cemetery office building, makes a cheerful  beginning to the uphill walk. What a view rewards the visitor who reaches the Sighthill plateau! It is worth a certain amount of huffing and puffing to get there. From this height, the surrounding tower blocks don't seem quite so assertive.

As previously mentioned, Springburn was once the locomotive-building capital of Europe. Now it bears little resemblance to the roaring, belching and clanging place it once was, surrounded instead with residential tower blocks painted in relaxing pastel shades.

On its smooth green hillock, framed by trees and bushes, Sighthill graveyard covers an extensive area, but the burial places in which we are interested are located on the central hill which is roughly oval in shape. Gravestones here are either obelisks, crosses or great hunks of stone. Only a few ever make you catch your breath (as on the Necropolis) or make you spontaneously exclaim 'Look at that!', but the people who lie beneath them are certainly worth examination. They could easily be the players in a pageant of the life and times of a younger, thrusting, more industrial Glasgow.

SIGHTHILL CEMETERY.

THE Public are invited to visit this beautiful Garden Cemetery, consisting of 50 Acres, more than half of which is already laid out in fine Walks and Parades, extending upwards of 4 miles. Its elevated situation and commanding views, with the picturesque beauty and various tastes displayed at immense cost in its embellishment, entitle it to its designation of the PERE LA CHAISE of Glasgow. From its extent, the Directors are enabled to accommodate themselves both to the taste and circumstances of every Purchaser, while, at the same time, a Nursery Garden, containing every variety of Plant suitable to the climate, is kept for supplying Purchasers with Flowers and Shrubs for the ornament of their burial-places.

Every encouragement is given to those desiring to erect Monuments. A handsome Chapel and Gateway are erected.

Apply to HILL, DAVIDSON, HILL, & CLARK, 1 South Frederick Street ; or Mr. COWAN, at the Cemetery.

COURTESY OF THE RCAHMS

Just to be awkward, we shall look first at the massive, red, granite stone of a man who built, not locomotives, but ships. Walk straight forward from the entrance gates about 120 paces until you come to where a path branches off to the

right. Turn right and walk 40 paces to where, above, on the left of the path, a grassy slope leads you up to the grave of [1] ROBERT CURLE (d1879, aged 66) under the shelter of some trees. Curle was building ships at Troon when he took the notion to

move in 1840. Meanwhile, a man called Robert Barclay was extending the shipbuilding business his father, John, had begun in 1818 at the Stobcross Pool near Partick. The two Roberts became partners, and in the following years their names became very well known to the Clydesiders.

Their names were a guarantee of the highest quality of shipbuilding. Their partnership was so bound in friendship that, if you look at the side of this stone, the middle name of Robert Curle's only son is Barclay.

Long after these men had passed away, their fine standards continued to live on in the company. In the desperate depression years of the early 1930s, when the Clyde shipyards stood idle and most of their workers were

unemployed, a club was formed for the men. Its purpose was to encourage them to take on jobs for friends or local businesses, using their skills to earn a shilling or two. Barclay, Curle & Company allowed the men to use their machine shops until Clydeside roused itself to building ships again.

Turn back down from the slope to the main road again, and then head on with the cemetery entrance still at your back. You will come to a fork where you can see [2] the MARTYRS' MONUMENT, around 120 paces immediately in front of you.

From the 1790s, and into the early decades of the 18th century, voices were raised across central Scotland claiming that the common people should have a say in the government of Scotland. By 1820, the voices were getting louder. After a skirmish at Bonnymuir in Stirlingshire, men were arrested and tried for treason. The most celebrated were John Baird and Andrew Hardie. They were executed at Stirling that year.

There is some doubt as to whether their bones lie beneath this well renovated stone, but it is here that they are regularly remembered. In August of 1820, James 'Pearlie' Wilson, a Strathaven weaver who marched to Cathkin Braes with a ragged group of innocuous 'revolutionaries', was arrested and made an example of. They hanged him in Jail Square, cut off his head and buried his remains in Fir Park near the Cathedral (the same Fir Park that later became the Necropolis).

Legend has it that, in the hours of darkness, Wilson's daughter and an aunt dug up the body and wheeled it back to Strathaven in a handcart for a decent Christian burial. Wilson's name was later added to this stone. There is an odd little fact about the Strathaven weaver — he got his nickname from having invented the 'pearl' stitch in knitting.

Go to the right of the fork at the Martyrs' Monument onto the path going up the hill and look out on the left (17 headstones up the slope) for the monument to the landscape painter [3] JOHN MILNE DONALD (1817-65).

Glasgow in the 19th century wasn't all crowded tenements and 'dark, satanic mills.' Much has been written about the celebrated Glasgow School of artists in the late decades of the century. But before WY Macgregor, James Guthrie and George Henry, there had been Sam Bough in the middle of the century who hailed from Carlisle. He really took centre stage at that time as Glasgow's landscape artist, and his fame lives on. He is buried at the fabulous Dean Cemetery in Edinburgh.

John Milne Donald was Bough's contemporary and some of his brilliant landscapes are in store at the People's Palace Museum. He was born in Nairn and, as a lad, came to Glasgow to be apprenticed to a house painter. His boss taught him how to copy pictures and in no time he was sketching his own interpretations of the Scottish landscape.

John Milne Donald spent some time in London as a picture restorer, but back in Glasgow he became a member of the newly formed West of Scotland Academy with whom his paintings were also exhibited. Death took him at the early age of forty-nine, but his work became a powerful influence on that later Glasgow School of landscape artists. Interestingly enough, one of Donald's greatest pictures is not really a landscape at all. Instead it is of the Town Hospital in Parliamentary Road.

Continue climbing up the road as it swings gently to the right. Soon you reach the broad path on the plateau, a path which runs along the long axis of that oval shape. Now turn left and head towards the circular walkway at the summit. When you reach it, on your left you will see the sad

remnants of a monument which was once a sight indeed!

There is no reason why attention would be drawn to the resting place of a gentleman called [4] FORREST and his wife MARGARET RISK, except that their memorial was made of cast-iron in the most intricate design which looked like the twin-towered roof of a church – the rest of the kirk having sunk out of sight below ground! Unhappily, over the past dozen or so years, the magnificent iron edifice has succumbed to vandalism and very little of it is left, only the solid base and one solitary iron urn, looking quite lost.

Now, go down the grassy path on the opposite side to the Risk memorial. It is steep – so be careful. When you reach the path below, turn sharp right and you find yourself face to face with the grave of the [5] MOSSMAN family. For generations the Mossmans were the foremost  monumental sculptors in Glasgow. John Mossman (d1914) was the son of John Snr, the firm's founder.

THE MOSSMAN SCULPTURE STUDIO, COURTESY OF JG MOSSMAN LTD

Few steps can be taken in Glasgow without encountering some Mossman sculpture. For instance, there are the figures of poetry, music and drama on the Citizens' Theatre façade, imposing torsos displayed with a flourish on many commercial buildings, and the impressive likenesses of Sir Robert Peel and Thomas Campbell (Glasgow's most famous poet) in George Square. But isn't it ironic that a family so famous for its stony twirls and convolutions, should be remembered here by a simple, unadorned block of granite?

Go back up the grass slope to the top path again. The circular path is now on the right. Turn to your left and walk down about 100 paces to where another path crosses at right angles. On your left are a number of ivy-covered obelisks. If the ivy did not obscure the words, you would be able to see that one of the stones was dedicated to the journalist **[6] JAMES HEDDERICK** (1814-97). Although sight of his memorial is today denied the visitor, stop and think about Hedderick. As owner and editor of *The Glasgow Evening Citizen*, he took note of the comments of a commercial traveller called John Brown who had written to the

newspaper deploring the fact that, almost a century after his birth, Glasgow had still not raised a suitable memorial to the world-famous poet Robert Burns.

Hedderick immediately set up an appeal for funds to do just that. He asked the people of Scotland to subscribe a shilling each. An amount of £2000 was gathered after a long campaign and, on 25 January 1877, a statue of Robert Burns was unveiled on the south side of George Square before the 'high heid yins' of the city. There is an interesting sub-plot in the story. It is said that also present at the unveiling was a man called Archie Campbell, the nephew of Highland Mary Campbell, who was the subject of some of Burns' finest verse. Mary had died of fever at Greenock in 1789.

Continue down the central path through the crossing. Fourteen stones down, in the second row of graves, a real locomotive man is remembered. Superintendent Engineer of the Caledonian Locomotive Company (founded in 1856), [7] BENJAMIN CONNER (1813-76) lived through the heyday of locomotive building. What marked Conner out from other engineers was that he added giant rear wheels onto his locomotives. They did not turn at such a great speed as the small ones at the front – but they travelled just as fast!

Nine graves further on in the same row is a reminder of another form of powered transport. The [8] Revd JAMES AITCHESON JOHNSTON (1822-95) was minister of Springburn United Presbyterian Church from 1861 until 1895. He died the year after. He was such a friend to his congregation that the church was later named Johnston Memorial. The manse was Mosesfield House in Springburn, a substantial dwelling. From this unexpected location, Scotland joined the motorcar business as the minister's son, George, was always inventing things, and one of his inventions in 1896 was a dog-cart. But not any old dog-cart – this one was driven by an internal combustion engine and was the first motorcar ever made in Britain. With financial backing from Sir William Arrol, George was to go on and build a number of models under the Arrol-Johnston name but the venture was eventually subsumed into other companies until its demise in 1931.

Now go directly to the path and walk 70 paces down it. On the right of the path you will see the 40-foot grey obelisk standing above the grave of [9] JAMES MOIR (1806-80). He was a rich city merchant, but his bank account never replaced his heart. Moir was one of the good people concerned for the welfare of his less fortunate fellow-creatures. He didn't shake the world with discoveries or feats of glory – his public service was as a 'Glesca toon cooncillor'. However, Moir read avidly and had a magnificent library and in 1878, just

three years before he died aged 74, he gave his entire collection of books to Glasgow's newly created Mitchell Library. He could never have guessed that he was helping to set up the institution which would become one of the finest reference libraries in Europe (and the largest). A hall in the Mitchell building is called after him. How lucky Glasgow has been to have its James Moirs.

Walk down another 30 paces and then go straight to the third row of stones on your left to find the Celtic cross of an important musical figure. It could be said that Sir Harry Lauder was Scotland's first international megastar. He, of course, would have been the first to admit that much of his success was due to the songs other people wrote for him. One of his songwriters was violinist and composer

[10] MACKENZIE MURDOCH (1870-1923), whose dark cross faces away from the path, to the houses at the edge of the cemetery. Sir Harry Lauder and Mackenzie Murdoch were born in the same year (1870). The former sang and told stories, the latter played the violin and strung words to music. Occasionally when Lauder was sailing to America to do a show, his ship was delayed by fog or icebergs. Homesick Scots waited in their Broadway theatre, often into the early hours of the morning, until Lauder arrived to perform for them the nostalgic song, 'Hame o' Mine'. It was Murdoch who wrote that famous song and not a dry eye was left in the theatre.

Sir Harry himself unveiled Murdoch's cross in September 1924. Those broken fixings at the base of the cross, by the way, once held a symbolic metal violin. Vandals ripped it off some time ago.

Return to the path, walk down 40 paces and you will see a great gloomy obelisk on your right, just where the path curves away down to the left. Here is [11] JAMES LAURIE (1790-1857), a Glasgow merchant. In his *Reminiscences of Glasgow*, Peter Mackenzie tells great stories about the Lauries. James Laurie, with his brother, owned a grain store in Union Street. The story goes that once, when the grain was packed up to the roof, water somehow got in and soaked it all. It was what you might call a *swell* affair. The grain expanded to about 50 times its original volume. Then Glasgow enjoyed a unique experience — a slow grain explosion! The store walls and the roof parted from each other in one great hideous eruption!

Go further down the path again, heading downhill, round the bend to the bottom of the end slope of the oval hill where, at the junction of two paths, [12] Professor WILLIAM LEIPER (d1867, aged 66) has an elegant stone

with a short pink granite column which once had a huge angel on top – probably now on someone's mantelpiece! The Professor had every right to be proud of his son, also called WILLIAM (1839-1916), who lies beside his father, a successful architect in the city. His work can still be seen, like the tall, red sandstone building at 153 St Vincent Street, and the Pearson Hall in Yorkhill Street, once used by the army and now residential flats, both of which are interesting examples.

Leiper's career spanned the last decades of the 19th century and the early years of the 20th, but he never really made the 'big time'. He missed his chance. In the early 1880s, Glasgow, recovering from the disastrous crash of the City of Glasgow Bank, wanted to cheer itself up by having a new City Chambers built in George Square. Architects were invited to take part in a design competition. All the greats entered –Burnet, Barry, Washington Browne, Sellars, Young and, of course, William Leiper.

Some jiggery pokery inevitably crept into the proceedings. William Young won, although on sheer technical merit, Browne should have taken the prize. Leiper, however, came in with a very attractive entry. It had a beautiful facade in 16th-century style and could have been a winner. But William had stuck a rather odd, unrelated tower on top. The judges thought it a bit of a joke and rejected it. William Leiper had missed his big chance.

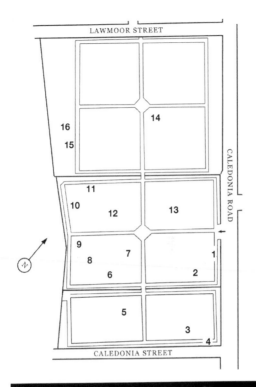

LAWMOOR STREET

CALEDONIA ROAD

16
15

14

11
10
12
13

9
8
7
6
1
2

5

3
4

CALEDONIA STREET

Southern Necropolis

300 Caledonia Road, GLASGOW G5 0TB
(administered by Glasgow City Council)
www.southernnecropolis.com

Caledonia Road runs from Crown Street in a roughly south-easterly direction and, some distance on, becomes Rutherglen Road. From Glasgow Cross go south along Saltmarket, cross the River Clyde over the Albert Bridge, continue on Crown Street and turn left into Caledonia Road. Not very far along, on the right hand side, is the Southern Necropolis lying in the shadow of the surrounding modern tower blocks, a real time capsule.

You enter under the magnificent stone gatehouse which resembles the gateway of a baronial castle. It would not look out of place with a drawbridge and portcullis. Immediately you see the graveyard shaded by mature trees, dominated by the over-arching foliage that covers the avenue leading from the entrance to the central turning point.

THE SOUTHERN
NECROPOLIS GATEHOUSE

In plan, the graveyard is a rectangle divided into three sections. The central section was laid out in 1840, the smaller east section in 1846; the west section (the largest of the three) dates from 1850. Within its outer walls the central and west sections have paths around their boundaries and centre paths running north/south and east/west. Each has a circular path in the middle.

The east section also has boundary paths and, where you enter from the central section, a single path dividing it in two. Solid stone walls separate the three sections. There are no intermediate paths. Visitors to graves located off the paths are expected to walk on the grass.

Having walked under the arch of the gatehouse, turn immediately left and look for a wall gravestone approximately 50 paces or 10 stones along. The man of substance interred here is the [1] Revd NATHANIEL PATERSON DD (1787-1871) who peeks out from under a swag of ivy – a Kirkudbright man who died in Helensburgh. The fact that Nathaniel wrote a book called *The Manse Garden* (Glasgow, 1836) would hardly be enough to win him immortality. His grandfather, Robert Paterson, however, certainly won an immortal memory because of his nickname – 'Old Mortality'.

Robert was a stonecutter who tramped all over Scotland repairing the graves of the Covenanters. 'Old Mortality' also featured in the first of Sir Walter Scott's *Tales of My Landlord*, collected and arranged by Jedediah Cleishbotham, schoolmaster and parish clerk of Gandercleugh (Edinburgh, 1816). This was the fourth volume of Scott's *The Waverley Novels*.

Walk south-east about 34 paces out from Nathaniel Paterson's stone over the central grassy area, then veer towards the dividing wall and path to your left. Look for three obelisks and one in  particular, a tall granite obelisk set on a square base. There you will find out about a man who mounted a full-scale attack on what was known as 'Scotland's curse' – drink.

By the middle of the 19th century, Glasgow had made a substantial liquid contribution towards the nation's drink problem but there were some notable exceptions such as the Temperance worker [2] PETER FERGUSON (d1885, aged 84) who was a missionary for many years with the Gorbals Total Abstinence Society. Those years brought the formation of all kinds of Temperance groups. Among them were the Good Templars, the British Women's Temperance Association, the Rechabites, the League of the Cross, the Sons of Scotland and (to the delight of Glasgow *weans* [kids] in the late decades of the 19th century, and well into the 20th century) the Band of Hope!

The *magic lantern* shows of the Band of Hope were indeed magic to the weans who came out of the dark streets into church halls all over the city. A series of coloured glass slides would show the plight of poor families suffering from the endless, heavy drinking of an uncaring father. When he ultimately repented, gave up the demon drink and became a loving husband and dad, the thunderous cheering of the Glasgow children reached a decibel pitch approaching that of a Hampden crowd when Scotland scores the winning goal. Only the penny matinées at the 'Pictures' (the cinema) on Saturdays could rival the popularity of the '*Bandy* Hope' among Glasgow's young folk.

The Scottish Band of Hope Union was founded in 1871 and Peter Ferguson was right in the thick of the activity. He founded Bands of Hope all over Glasgow. He spent much of his life in the midst of hope and faith, but probably never guessed that the movement he helped found would turn out such a success and last for so long. But eventually, even the Band of Hope lost its popularity – just like the penny matinée.

Now go up to that centre gap which lies under a large tree and through the opening in the wall that divides the central and east sections. Walk down the central path of the east section to the east boundary wall. Turn left and walk about 75 paces towards the north-east corner. About three-quarters of the way along, step left onto the grass and look for the tall, polished stone with a horizontal block of granite in front of it. It is just beside the path and faces west.

The grandest of Glasgow grocers, [3] Sir THOMAS LIPTON (1850-1931) lies here. For generations, Glaswegians recovered from, and faced up to, all kinds of crises by brewing a soothing cup of Lipton's Tea. It made the man into a legend. His Belfast ham (a ham with a unique taste, first soaked in brine and then smoked with peat) was reckoned to be the food of the gods. His Irish Protestant father opened a grocer's shop at Crown Street in 1849 and Thomas was born in the Gorbals the following year.

After learning the trade from his father, Lipton cut the family ties and opened his own provisions shop in Anderston on his 21st birthday. His grocery empire would become world-famous. Glasgow schoolboys chanted:

Why does Lipton wear green braces? Guess! You silly pup!
Oh, Lipton wears green braces for to keep his trousers up!
That's not why he wears green braces! No, you stupid clown!
He wears them on his trousers for to stop them falling down!

Sir Thomas's lifelong passion was sailing yachts. He commissioned five huge racers – all called *Shamrock* – with which he tried repeatedly to win the Americas' Cup. He never did, but he had rare fun trying to …

Walk on about 38 paces to the far north-east corner of this east section: a gravestone offers an unusual invitation to read a book. The stone bears the name of [4] Sergeant JAMES RESTON (d1834, aged 63), late of the 94th Scotch Brigade Regiment of Foot. But the real interest surrounds his wife AGNES HARKNESS, who also lies here. On this stone she is called the 'Heroine of Matagorda', a fort on the outskirts of the Spanish city of Cadiz.  During the Peninsular War, under two months' heavy bombardment from a large French force, Agnes helped to care for the wounded and carried water and other supplies even though wounded herself.

The inscription states that details of her heroism may be found in fellow soldier Joseph Donaldson's *Recollections of the Eventful Life of a Soldier* (Edinburgh, 1852). In his 'A Humble Heroine' the poet William Topaz McGonagall makes use of the story, describing the courage of Agnes Harkness:

*And while the shells shrieked around, and their fragments
did scatter,
She was serving the men at the guns with wine and water;
And while the shot whistled around, her courage wasn't
slack,
Because to the soldiers she carried sand-bags on her back.*

After her husband's death Agnes at first was obliged to
live in the Glasgow Poorhouse, until a public appeal raised
enough money to give her a modest pension for life. She
finally died in 1856, aged 85.

Next, retrace your steps towards the
gap in the wall by which you entered.
In the third last row of stones, nine
graves from the cobbled road, is the
stone you are looking for. It faces
south, half-sunk into the ground and
marks the last resting place of [5]
JOHN BEGG, son of Isabel Begg. John
was the nephew of a famous uncle –
Robert Burns. His mother Isabel was
the youngest sister of the great Scottish poet. She was 11
years old and on her way home from a sewing class, when
she was unexpectedly asked to stand in as partner for a boy
at Tarbolton Dancing School. There she saw her brother
Robert dancing with Ellison (also known as Alison) Begbie,
a local farmer's daughter. Burns was very fond of Ellison
but she did not return his feelings. The
song Burns wrote with Ellison in mind
does not mention her name, but Isabel
Begg later revealed to those writing
the biography of her brother, that one
of his finest songs, although called
'Mary Morison', was really about
Ellison Begbie. Isabel told quite a bit
of the 'inside' story of the poet. She
made 'kiss and tell' revelations. If she

had lived in this century, the tabloids would have loved her! Her son John died in 1867, aged 71. His son Matthew was buried here 30 years later.

Now pass through the gap back into the central section and then turn left. Take a few strides towards the south wall, then turn right and walk over the grass for twenty paces until you reach a solid granite monument in the third row, lying on its back. The name of the **[6] Revd JAMES ELISHAMA SMITH** (d1857, aged 55) is inscribed here under that of his father John Smith, a merchant in the city. James Smith packed a lot of work into his years. He was nicknamed 'Shepherd' Smith after a journal by that name that he edited. He wrote articles for the weekly *Family Herald* and also edited another paper called *Crisis* for Robert Owen, at his cotton mill in New Lanark. Some people regarded Smith as a prophet

and were devotees of his *The Divine Drama of History and Civilisation* (London, 1854). Smith also published his *Family Herald* articles in book form.

Walk around 60 paces to the large Corinthian column close to the turning circle of the central section and then go south to the third-last stone in the row, the grave of the prominent Glasgow policeman, **[7] Superintendent JAMES SMART** (d1870, aged 66). Smart was no softie. The 19th century was barely four years old when James was born.

Since he died in 1870, he must have held office through some very turbulent times.

He worked at the Gorbals Police Station. Before his arrival there, it was notorious for one particularly ghastly incident in the late 1820s which brought disgrace on an earlier Police Superintendent. This *Master of Police*, as the title was then, was one Mr Clark, a cast-iron disciplinarian and Sabbatarian who thought that even to breathe on a Sunday was sinful.

A young Paisley weaver had come to Glasgow for a Saturday night out, got drunk, fought with some ruffians who tried to rob him, and was arrested. While manacled in Gorbals Police Station he fell into an open fire. His blood-curdling screams brought some worthy citizens rushing in to find out what the trouble was. Clark and his surly turnkeys threw them out. Some people went back on Sunday when they heard a man had been burned but Clark locked them up for the night. When they were released the next day, they heard that the young weaver had died. Mr Clark denied any knowledge of the incident.

But the callous Master of Police got his come-uppance. There was such an outcry that he was removed from his job and the powers of the local Gorbals magistrates were transferred to Glasgow's Lord Provost and magistrates. From that time onwards Glasgow's Master of Police also took over all the administration of the law on the south side of the city.

James Smart, however, held the position of Police Superintendent for many years, and though he used some pensioned-off soldiers to fire on the crowds during the Bread Riots of the 1840s, he seems otherwise to have been firm but fair. He was appointed Chief Constable of Glasgow in 1862 and made a number of important improvements: he introduced the Mounted Branch, replaced the police rattle with a whistle and the police stick with a baton. Smart also brought in a system of magnetic telegraph communication between police and fire stations.

Turn and walk south for 50 paces. Then turn left for another 20 paces and look in the grass for a small stone shaped like a scroll. It lies a few metres from the south path and marks the grave of [8] HUGH MACDONALD (1817-1860), author of the most popular book ever written about the city, *Rambles Around Glasgow* (1854). In the middle of the 19th century, 'male chauvinist' clubs were at the height of fashion. Hugh Macdonald was a member of the City Club that met in the Bank Tavern at the Trongate. There the literary giants of Glasgow expounded their theories on improving and saving the world. Hugh was not slow to offer advice to young men thinking about getting married. He advised one young fellow not to bother so much about how a lassie looked, but to scrutinise carefully the kind of washing she hung on her line. A clean, fresh washing was worth getting married for!

Next up is an interesting coincidence – it was a chance visit to Helensburgh in 1811 that ensured a place in history for two shipbuilding brothers, John and Charles Wood of Port Glasgow. On a summer Saturday afternoon in Helensburgh, Henry Bell invited them to build him a steamship. It was to be called the *Comet* and would be the first steamship to sail on the Clyde. The Woods decided to take the job and their company went on to become a steaming success.

The three-horsepower engine for the *Comet* (the first steamboat that plied regularly in Europe) was supplied by Glaswegian [9] JOHN ROBERTSON (1782-1868). Under a tree, some 30 paces to the southwest, his grave can be found down nearer to the south path of the central section, over towards the path running from the main gatehouse entrance to the south boundary wall. A magnificent bronze portrait head and commemorative plaque fixed in 1912 to the gravestone by the Institute of Engineers and Shipbuilders records the part Robertson played in producing the *Comet*.

Henry Bell, by the way, was not particularly well off when he ventured on his historic project. Indeed, he never paid the Wood brothers' bill for building his steamship – a sum of £100. And he continued to owe £52 to John Robertson as part-payment for the engine. Perhaps these gentlemen did not demand payment because in their bones they could feel that the new era was going to make them 'fairy-tale' rich. They were right.

Move now to the south path of the central section and walk west for around 90 paces, past the centre path, and then down towards the corner. Look out on the right for a large stone lying on its back. Only the base remains where it was first set. Members of the [10] GEDDES family lie here. The three George Geddes made up a formidable dynasty. In 1787, James Coulter, a Glasgow merchant, left £200 to the Royal College of Physicians and Surgeons of Glasgow, to be used to set up facilities for the rescue and recovery of drowning persons. Thus, in 1790, the Glasgow Humane Society was founded; five years later a house for the Society Officer and a boathouse, had been built by the Clyde on Glasgow Green.

Geordie Geddes became the Society Officer in 1857 and held the post until he died, aged 63, in 1889. His son, also called 'Geordie' by Glaswegians, was Officer from his father's death until 1932.

Drama filled their lives. They were constantly on call to rescue people from the Clyde. Sometimes it was victims of accidents, but more often those who had jumped from a bridge in a bid to commit suicide. The recovery of dead bodies, and sometimes murder weapons, was also part of the Geddes' grim profession.

The third George Geddes, grandson to the original Geordie, joined the rescue business when he gained the Diploma of the Royal Humane Society at 17. On a dreary day in November 1928, young Geordie dived into the Clyde to rescue a man who had jumped from St Andrew's Suspension Bridge. The struggle with the fellow determined to end his own life was desperate. This time young Geordie did not succeed and both drowned in the dark, cold waters of the Clyde. The whole of Glasgow was plunged into mourning

ST ANDREW'S
SUSPENSION BRIDGE

for that brave young man. He was just 37. The base of the Geddes stone bears the inscription relating to young Geordie's death.

The Geddes family did a job that inevitably made legends of them. It also made a legend of their successors, Ben Parsonage (1903-79) and his son, George. The Glasgow Humane Society is very special to this city which always raises its *bunnet* [cap] to courage. It is probably the last society of its kind in the world and the oldest practical society.

Some 90 paces west of the Geddes grave and a little north (on the wall dividing the central section from the west section) is the gravestone of Pollokshaws master carpenter [11] ALLAN GLEN (1772-1850), who rose to become a

Glasgow burgess, a prosperous property developer and philanthropist. His stone is on the wall dividing the central section from the west section. Glen died three years before the opening of the famous Glasgow school that bears his name which became renowned for its success in science-based subjects. Allan Glen kept good company – Stephen Mitchell (the tobacco manufacturer who left money to found the Mitchell Library); George Baillie (of the famous Baillie

Institution) and William Teacher (the whisky producer). Like Glen, they were all members of the Unitarian Church.

The ground for a new Unitarian Church at St Vincent Street and Pitt Street was acquired under the patronage of William Teacher and Thomas Laidlaw, a local Customs official. There was a spirited team if ever there was one! The triangular site of the church presented no real problems for architect JT Rochead who designed a building in the Greek style – perhaps it was Greek because it was a triangular site and some gesture had to be made to Pythagoras and his famous theorem ('The square of the hypoteneuse ...')? That would really have pleased the meticulous craftsman that was Allan Glen. In April 1856, only six years after Glen's death, the church opened with no great pomp or ceremony.

Now visitors should know that in the Southern Necropolis there is something much more disturbing as we move from craftsmanship to a very different story – *Road Accident and Haunting*! For the last few decades Gorbals children have come to this graveyard hoping to experience the tingling joy of being terrified by the *White Lady* who is said to turn her head as you pass her by! Walk diagonally for around forty paces across the grass from Allan Glen's stone, heading again towards that centre circle of the central section, and the White Lady is right

there: [12] MAGDALENE SMITH (not to be confused with Madeleine Smith, see Pierre Émile L'Angelier, page 80), wife of carpet manufacturer John S Smith. Magdalene died at the age of 85 alongside her 55-year-old housekeeper, Mary McNaughton. On 29 October 1933, a dark, wet Sunday evening, they were both knocked down

by a tramcar in Queen's Drive on their way home from church. Magdalene died on arrival at the Victoria Infirmary while Mary McNaughton lived on for two more weeks before finally passing away. Mary McNaughton was so much part of the family that mistress and servant were not separated in death. They lie here together, with the White Lady standing upright by the stone that bears their names. On misty mornings children on their way to school can see through the railings of the graveyard. Perhaps they wonder if it is a strand of mist floating at the far side ... or the White Lady ... silently gliding past?

Go across the path that runs west to east in front of you. Around 80 paces north-east of the White Lady, about halfway between the cross path and the north boundary wall, you will find [13] WILLIAM ROBB (d1884, aged 68). There is no special reason to remember him, but his

gravestone simply has to be seen to be believed. The base is formed from two dull rectangular blocks supporting a semi-circular top. Crowning the semi-circle is a huge urn, ridiculously out of proportion with the base. Indeed, if the urn were turned upside-down, it might almost be an inter-continental ballistic missile!

A few of his friends contributed towards the cost of the memorial. Did they mean it as a joke? Perhaps William Robb has already looked down upon the monstrosity and mused 'My friends ... you must be kidding!' It is surely the ugliest gravestone in Glasgow.

Go through into the west section. It has the same cross-shaped path layout as the central section. Walk towards the centre circle and before you reach it, you will notice on the right the gravestone of the Brown family. Two steps further

on is a glistening modern memorial to [14] ALEXANDER 'GREEK' THOMSON (1817-75) erected by the Glasgow Institute of Architects (a body Thomson helped to found). Thomson was the 17th of 20 children, and became one of the leading Glasgow architects of the 19th century. In 2006 the polished,

Irish, black granite memorial was unveiled by the Lord Provost of Glasgow in the presence of members of the Thomson family.

The United Presbyterians engaged 'Greek' Thomson to design their new church to be built on a hilly site at St Vincent Street. He created a design that used Egyptian, Greek, Roman (and even Indian) features that helped to earn him his nickname of 'Greek'. Architectural experts believe that he probably had Jerusalem and Solomon's Temple in mind. On the opening day in 1859 crowds thronged to it and the inaugural collection taken amounted to a staggering £402 (around £25,000 today!). Take a look at his Grosvenor Building in Gordon Street (facing Central Station), and his masterpiece, the Egyptian Halls building in Union Street which is partly cast-iron. It is a wonderful fusion of all Thomson's favourite styles.

Go on to the centre circle path and then turn south to the path that runs parallel to the south boundary wall. There are two rows of graves on the edge of the broad grassy margin between the path and the wall. Turn left and look out on the right for a stone with the images of an old-fashioned police helmet, a treble clef and a musical instrument on it, symbols for the busy life of [15] CHARLES THOMSON (d1899, aged 32), a member of the Glasgow Police Silver Band. He must have been looking forward to joining the fanfare as the  bandsmen played themselves into the new century, but they had to march into it without him.

Come back now a few paces to a gap in the double line of graves. Turn onto that broad grassy margin. The back line of gravestones faces south. Move along to a stone almost directly behind the grave of the police musician.

Glasgow in the 19th century was not short of 'characters'. They were the street people who scraped a living from performing daft tricks, singing, or making music on all kinds of instruments such as [16] Wee WILLIE WHITE, a blind man who played the flute and flageolet around the Glasgow streets in the 1840s and 50s, with a fair degree of skill. He was a squat man, and always seemed to have an expression of quiet thoughtfulness – even when he was playing lively tunes. One admirer said that Willie earned enough to keep himself in 'respectable poverty'.

WEE WILLIE WHITE, COURTESY COLIN MACKIE

His Glasgow audiences loved him. They have a habit of taking kindly to underdogs. And so, people were shocked when news spread through the streets that Wee Willie had been taken ill as he tootled one afternoon on Glasgow Green and had died at his Saltmarket lodging that very evening in September 1858. Apparently no one knew what age he was when he died. Good friends arranged his burial here and had the stone erected. The carving on it is said to represent his favourite musical instrument and the box he carried it in. A fair stretch of the imagination is needed to see it that way. It looks more like a coal-fire, a luxury that Wee Willie White could never have afforded.

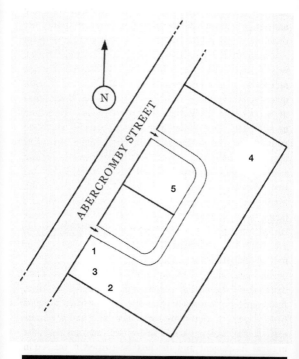

Calton Burying Ground

Abercromby Street, GLASGOW G40 1NQ
www.scotcip.org.uk/weaving_yarns.html

The name 'Calton' has one pronunciation in Glasgow and another in some parts of Edinburgh. Some Edinburghers say '*Caw*-lton' – Glaswegians say *Cahl*-ton. To reach this old graveyard (1787), travel east from Glasgow Cross along Gallowgate until the crossing with Bellgrove Street on the left and Abercromby Street on the right. Turn right into Abercromby Street and go almost to the end where you will see the high wall and the iron gate of the burial ground.

In summer the cemetery is a quiet haven, full of wild flowers and birds. But the present peacefulness hides a much less tranquil past. Throughout the 18th and much of the 19th century weaving was a mainstay of the economy of the village of Calton. For a time during the first half of the 19th century, the village was a barony or *burgh*. Its coat of arms displayed three cats holding shuttles (the tool of the weaver's trade) in their mouths. Manufacturers supplied the raw material which local craftsmen then wove at home. Eventually the Weaver Trade Society of Calton was founded, a master weaver's organisation which was really a kind of friendly society.

They bought this area for a burial ground which opened in May 1787 and another section was added in 1822. Journeymen weavers were not, of course, members of this society, so their families had to buy lairs in the graveyard.

A reading of the burial records of the Calton Burying Ground shows something of the state of medical science in those early years. Causes of death make interesting reading – croup, cough, cholera, fever, burning, bowel-bind, childbed, water on brain, 'decline'.

However, just a month or so after the opening of the graveyard, a crisis overtook the weaving trade in Glasgow. The East India Company was importing cheap Indian muslins. This, in November 1786, had caused a price drop in Scottish cloth and a six to seven shilling cut in weavers' wages. The manufacturers announced that further wage cuts would be made in June 1787. On the last day of that month, thousands of weavers held a meeting on Glasgow Green and resolved not to work for what would be starvation wages.

The strike dragged on for three months. The plight of the weavers' families became more and more desperate. Some broke ranks and took on work at the low rate, and were attacked by the men still holding out. The Lord Provost of Glasgow and his magistrates received word on 3 September that a crowd was ripping cloth from the looms of the strike-breakers. Down they went to Calton to intervene, only to be pelted with bricks! Up came intimidating reinforcements in the shape of the 39th Regiment of Foot commanded by Lieutenant-Colonel Kellet. There was a short pitched battle before the soldiers fired into the crowd. Three weavers were shot dead and three were mortally wounded. Others suffered superficial wounds. But the sporadic fighting soon died out and the strike was broken.

Three of the dead weavers [1] JOHN PAGE, ALEXANDER MILLER and JAMES AINSLEY, were buried here together, just to the south of the entrance to the south section, and by the outer wall. Over 6,000 people attended the funeral.

The walls had not then been completed around the graveyard, so it was possible for the mass of mourners to spread right round the grave. Two plaques on the wall tell the story of that dreadful day of strife.

Of the other three weavers, it is said that one was buried in the Ramshorn, one in the Gorbals, and the other in some unknown location.

From the weavers' grave, move over to the south boundary wall and look for the polished grey granite stone of one [2] JOHN MONTGOMRIE (d1908, aged 79) and his wife, ELIZA HAMILTON (d1901, aged 81). It is just a few metres along from the corner. These two are not particularly famous, but have a strong claim to be remembered here.

John Montgomerie was an engineer with the Caledonian

Railway in Perth and he and Eliza were married for 58 years. The quality of their married life seems to have been unaffected by Eliza being fully nine years older than John. Today, in a society which offers all kinds of agencies and resources for marriage guidance, it might be worth reflecting upon what supported John and Eliza through all the years of their marriage. For it is clearly stated here on the stone – *Psalm 23*. The Lord was their Shepherd. They did not want. Surely goodness and mercy followed them all the days of their lives.

Just a few steps out from the south wall, and nearer the weavers' grave, an obelisk is a poignant reminder that in Glasgow the graves of young divinity students of the 19th century are encountered with sad regularity. Such was [3] ROBERT MITCHELL (d1846, aged 20), scarcely out of his teens. The 1840s were years ridden with famine and disease – demons that were not selective in their choice of victim. They spared neither saint nor sinner.

Go along the path at the edge of the partition wall into the north section and, up close to the north-east corner, look for the [4] MUSHET family plot where once a modest memorial to another divinity student was visible – JAMES MUSHET (d1819, aged 24), who died on Midsummer's Day. That was a summer when there were more rumbles of social discontent than thunder clouds. There was a time when you could read the inscription on young Jamie's gravestone. It gave pause for some thought: 'That life is long which answers life's great end.'

Walk back along the diagonal line from the north-east corner of the north section to the south-west corner. Cross the path and look out for another obelisk memorial. It will be of particular interest to Scotland's American cousins when they visit the city.

Doctor of Divinity the [5] Revd JAMES SMITH (1798-1871) was born the son of a Glasgow couple, Peter and Margaret Smith. James Smith was one divinity student who survived to undertake a ministry of 40 years abroad in America where he was pastor to President Abraham Lincoln. He returned to Scotland before the end of the American Civil War, but so high a regard did Lincoln have for him that he appointed James Smith as the US Consul in Scotland. His office was in Dundee.

You can almost imagine the old minister experiencing such joy when he heard that the Civil War was over; but then grief – when he learned how the fanatic actor, JW Booth, had fatally wounded President Lincoln with one shot as he sat in a theatre box on the evening of 14 April 1865.

When he died, only six years later, James Smith was brought home to lie here in the Calton Burying Ground.

Jocelyn Square G1 5JU

The visitor looking for Jocelyn Square has to walk down the Saltmarket from Glasgow Cross, to the wide space between the imposing austerity of the Justiciary Courts and the main entrance to the paths and pleasures of Glasgow Green. Jocelyn Square is not really a square, but an open area in front of Glasgow's most famous park, with the main road carrying heavy traffic north and south across the River Clyde. It is a pleasant place nevertheless, with some glorious displays of flowers in spring and summer.

Once it was called Jail Square. Today it is named more happily after the wise old bishop who founded Glasgow Fair. Indeed, this was once the setting of the thrills and spills of the fair as showmen vied to win customers by offering breathtaking and exotic attractions. The square also had a more sombre use – public hangings were regularly carried out there. A stranger would surely never guess that close by this bright, busy place, there was a graveyard. But there is. Some of the people hanged there were buried just over to the north of the Court buildings, where the City Mortuary now stands.

When the foundations for the mortuary were being dug some years ago, the remains of one of Glasgow's most notorious killers were found. He was an eminent, much-respected doctor with a fashionable practice in Sauchiehall Street. He was 40-year-old Dr EDWARD PRITCHARD (d1865). Mother of five children, Mary Jane Pritchard was the victim of her husband, the 'The Human Crocodile' who, with tartarised antimony, poisoned first his mother-in-law and then his 38-year-old wife. When his mother-in-law died in Edinburgh, Dr Pritchard callously came through from Glasgow for the funeral.

Later, as his wife lay in her coffin at her parents' home in Edinburgh, Dr Pritchard made a show of bending down to kiss the lifeless corpse. But the police eventually became suspicious, exhumed the mother-in-law's body and found it to be full of antimony. Dr Pritchard was arrested and tried at the High Court in Edinburgh. Respectable Glaswegians were stunned when the doctor was arrested and tried for the poisonings – there was also a suspicion that he had disposed of a maid as well.

Pritchard was found guilty of murder and sentenced to be hanged on 28 July 1895 in Glasgow's Jail Square, the last public execution in the city of Glasgow. On that day in 1865, people came from all directions and great distances to be in at the kill. They turned the occasion into a kind of jamboree. Thousands filled the square and the surrounding streets. Traders set up stalls to provide food and drink. To enthusiasts who wanted a grandstand view of Dr Pritchard's final moments the people living in the tenements around the Square hired their windows out at three guineas per spectator.

As he came out here between two of his jailers and looked around, Dr Pritchard expressed his disgust at this outrageous display of bad taste by the Glasgow crowd.

Many years later, when his bones were brought to light during the excavations, it appeared that he was still wearing his boots. It is rumoured that someone took them as souvenirs!

Be sure that some of Dr Edward Pritchard still lies, with the bones of others, beneath that mortuary ...

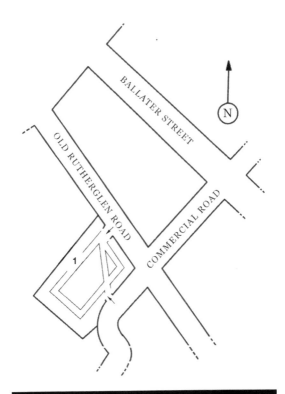

Gorbals Cemetery

Old Rutherglen Road, GLASGOW G5 0QZ

Now known as Gorbals Rose Garden, the cemetery (opened in 1715 and extended in 1807) is not far from the Southern Necropolis. Travel south from Glasgow Cross, down the Saltmarket, cross the Albert Bridge over the Clyde, continue on Crown Street and turn left into Ballater Street. A short distance on, turn right into Commercial Road, and the cemetery can be seen straight ahead. The main entrance is in Old Rutherglen Road.

Today, Glasgow City Council has tidied up the debris caused by time, weather and vandalism, and the cemetery is now a pleasant public garden full of bushes and flowers. There are still gravestones to be seen. Some show the tools of the artisans who lie here. But, about 100 paces from the entrance, halfway down the path, look right and you will see the stone on the west wall which marks the grave of a man who caused Robert Burns much irritation.

In 1785 [1] JOHN WILSON (d1839, aged 88) was the parish schoolteacher at Tarbolton, but the dominie also added to his earnings by running a small grocery shop. More than that, he sold pharmaceutical drugs as well as food, and had a card in his shop window which advertised free 'medical advice'!

In the spring of that year Burns spent an evening in the company of the dominie. John talked on for hours, explaining that he was so skilled in medicine and surgery that even Hippocrates would have been proud of him! Burns was certainly glad to bid him farewell and get out into the fresh air of the spring night. And as the poet walked back home to Mossgiel, the muse came whispering in his ear.

The result was his outrageously funny poem, 'Death and Doctor Hornbook', which swept John Wilson into immortality. It tells how Burns, as he strolled in the moonlight, came face to face with Death who was in a capricious mood. Death at first complained to the bard about

Dr Hornbook's (really John Wilson's) magic medicines. Ironically, the Grim Reaper said that they were so effective, he was being denied his normal harvest of human flesh! But, after letting out a blood-curdling guffaw, Death admitted that Hornbook was in fact killing more patients than he, Death, could handle!

> *An honest wabster to his trade,*
> *Whase wife's twa nieves were scarce weel-bred,*
> *Gat tippence-worth to mend her head,*
> *When it was sair;*
> *The wife slade cannie to her bed,*
> *But ne'er spak mair.*

When the kirk clock chimed an early hour, Burns parted from Death, with his mind as sharp and clear as the night air.

John Wilson moved to Glasgow shortly afterwards because of a dispute over his salary in Tarbolton. He continued as a teacher until he took over the position of Session Clerk in Gorbals parish. Until his death he prospered. And he was first to admit that his prosperity was due, in large part, to the interest caused by being the subject of those famous, rather mischievous verses by Robert Burns. Wilson's daughter also lies in this grave. She died in 1824, aged 28. Her first name seems to have been 'Campbell'.

Give thought now also to ROBERT HALL (d1843). Liken a Glaswegian to *Rab Ha'* and you're in trouble. For Rab Ha' was the celebrated 'Glesga Glutton'. He displayed his addiction to food around the city about the middle of the 19th century. His guzzling was such entertainment that people actually paid for the food he shovelled down his gullet!

He would sometimes leave the city to entertain the populace in the country. There were barns there big enough to house him. If the *Guinness Book of Records* had been published in Rab's day, he would have earned a place in it for his supreme performance. One day, for a wager, he actually ate a whole calf at one sitting!

Sadly Rab Ha' was found dead one day in a hayloft on

Thistle Street, right here in the Gorbals. Ponder for a while on this extraordinary fellow, and scan slowly around this quadrangle of everlasting rest. For somewhere in here lies Rab Ha' – his final resting place unmarked.

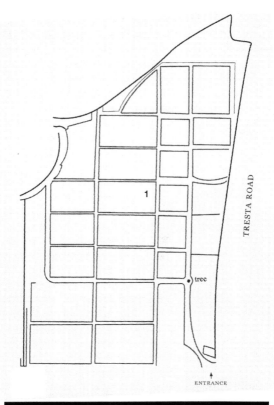

TRESTA ROAD

• tree

↑
ENTRANCE

St Kentigern's

951 Balmore Road, GLASGOW G23 5HA

Officially, St Kentigern's and the Western Necropolis are separate cemeteries but in reality they are ecumenically side-by-side, so a visit to both can easily be combined. From the city centre the journey takes you across the M8 at junction 16, out through the north side of Glasgow along the A879 by way of Saracen Street and Balmore Road. After crossing the Forth & Clyde Canal turn left into Skirska Street just before the city limits. Then take the second right into Tresta Road. You will find the cemetery down the road on your right.

Row upon row of gravestones slope up into the horizon, as far as the eye can see. A huge host of white angels and saints give the place a touch of Italian or French – a bit like St Peter's cemetery in the south-east, but more open.

Walk up, taking the main road from the entrance which curves up to the right. Walk on till you reach a mini-roundabout with a large dead tree in the middle. Take the left turn and then the first right. At the third access path to your left go in to the second row of gravestones. Here you will find a substantial standing stone facing away from you to the hills on the horizon.

Here (in Section 15) is the grave of yet another Glasgow legend, his name written in letters of gold. Many sit in pubs and clubs still claiming even the most tenuous link with

boxer [1] BENNY LYNCH (1913-46). Even having a granny whose milkman once met the wee champ is a valid enough boast.

The Lynch family came from Ireland in the late 19th century, at a time when the poverty endured over there made the notion of moving to Glasgow seem like a trip to the Promised Land.

They settled in the Gorbals where Benny Lynch was born. Life was a struggle for most people in the Gorbals back then, but Benny had something to offer. He showed the local boxing fraternity that he could fight for his living in the ring – better than most of the lads in the game.

Around the booths and boxing arenas, his reputation grew, and, by the mid-thirties he had taken the flyweight crown from Jackie Brown in Manchester. The Americans, however, did not recognise him as undisputed world flyweight champion until he had beaten their lad, Small Montana, in London in 1936.

Glasgow went quite hysterical over its new world champion – the first that Scotland had ever had. Citizens claimed that his fists travelled faster than the speed of light! He was never allowed to escape from the glaring spotlight of publicity or entertainment.

But alas, within a year or so, the demon drink began to take the fine, sharp edge off the champ. His training was not going well and fat was growing around his muscles. In June 1938, he was due to defend his title against the American, Jackie Jutich, at Shawfield Park. Now it happened that, at this time, the bridge which carried trains from the Central Station across the Clyde had a huge advertisement plastered across it. The ad was for a well-known cheap wine and it claimed that there were 'six-and-a-half pounds of grapes in every bottle'.

At the weigh-in before the big fight, the unfortunate Benny Lynch was found to be exactly *six-and-a-half pounds overweight*. Naturally the cynics made a lot of the coincidence. The weight gain had cost Lynch his title. The fight went on at *catch-weights* with no title at stake. Ironically Lynch won easily, but from then on his journey was downhill. The drink was beating him. Sir Harry Lauder, a keen supporter of boxing, tried to talk Benny into giving up drink. But the wee fellow told him, 'I was born in the gutter and I'll die in the gutter'.

One July evening in 1946, at a particularly dull boxing gala in Hampden Park, the fans were booing and on the point of leaving when Benny Lynch shuffled down to a ringside seat someone had bought for him. When he was spotted, thunderous cheering swept round the arena in a warm tribute to him. It was his last ovation. He died days later on 6 August 1946.

This stone, erected by his fans, looks over to the Campsie Fells where Benny jogged, training for his fights. The black polished stone bears an etched likeness of him in boxing gear and calls him the 'Undefeated World Flyweight Champion'.

This is not strictly true perhaps. He was defeated – by the broken parts of his personality, by the relentless adoration, by life itself. But in the folk memory of this city, Benny Lynch will always be undefeated.

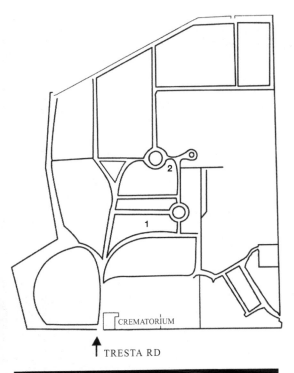

CREMATORIUM

↑ TRESTA RD

Western Necropolis

19 Tresta Road, GLASGOW G23 5LB

Adjacent to St Kentigerns' cemetery is the Western Necropolis and Lambhill Cemetery with its red brick crematorium chapel. The Cemetery Office is through the entrance gates and it faces back uphill to the cemetery itself.

Walk forward from the gates for a hundred paces, following the main drive up to a large tree. Then take the second road to your right. Follow it for 90 paces as it rises towards the trees ahead. Halfway up, on your left, two rows of stones back from the road (in lair *K401*), you will see the

pink granite stone of [1] Sir WILLIAM SMITH (1854 -1914), facing down towards you and the crematorium. Also buried here are his father, mother and sister.

William Alexander Smith is well known as the founder (1883) of the Boys' Brigade *(BB)* in Glasgow from the Sunday School of the North Woodside Mission. His timing was perfect. The lads of the city were in need of meaningful activity and 28 of them rushed to join when invited.

So many boys in the tenement canyons of the city at that time had nowhere to belong to. The 'BB' put some purpose into their lives. There were games to play, crafts to learn, a uniform to wear, drilling and marching to smarten them up — even wooden rifles to play soldiers with. The rifles were later withdrawn when some folk complained that the organisation seemed a bit too militaristic.

But hundreds and, later, thousands of boys were to have their way of life transformed by joining the Boys' Brigade. They discovered too that they did not meet once a week for fun alone. They would learn that a boy was nearer to becoming a man when he washed some old lady's windows, rather than when he threw stones through them. He would be taught the kind of behaviour that makes Christian principles real.

But William Alexander Smith was not unrealistic. It is said that he believed there was more promise in a Boy daft enough to stick a pin in his pal for a lark,

SIR WILLIAM SMITH, COURTESY OF THE BOYS' BRIGADE

than there was in a Boy pious as an angel! Interestingly, Captain Smith always spelt the word 'Boy' with a capital 'B'.

Smith's Boys' Brigade grew to become a successful worldwide organisation to which he dedicated his life. World War I was within a few months of breaking out and he was just short of his 60th birthday, when he took ill suddenly at a meeting in London. He died in St Bartholomew's Hospital on 10 May 1914.

The entire movement was shocked by the news. Four thousand Boys marched into London's St Paul's Cathedral for the memorial service on the following Friday. All the organisations who saluted him as their pioneer sent their leaders – the Church Lads' Brigade, the Catholic Boys' Brigade, the London Diocesan Church Lads' Brigade, the Jewish Boys' Brigade, the Boys' Life Brigade, and the Boy Scouts who came with their leader, Sir Robert Baden-Powell.

The night train from London's Euston Station brought the founder's body home for burial in Glasgow, a city in mourning. Seven thousand Boys lined the route as the cortège came slowly towards the Western Necropolis. Thousands of men, women and children followed. Boys of his 1st Glasgow Company filed past the open grave, each casting a white flower into it.

The *BB* has changed with the times. It is no longer restricted to shrill bugles and skirling pipes. It makes all kind of music now – martial, classical, jazz, rock, folk, you name it.

It is also a far cry from the early summer camps at Kilchattan Bay on Bute, where some Glasgow lads saw the sea for the first time. It is said that one wee lad rushed to tell the captain the sea had been stolen – it was just that the tide had gone out. Summer trips nowadays can mean anywhere in the world. If Sir William is watching his Boys' Brigade marching smartly towards the 22nd century, surely he is smiling.

Continue now to the first road leading off to the left and up the hill. Take it through one mini-roundabout to the top of the hill to another roundabout. Turn left to a larger roundabout. On its southern edge is a small scroll-shaped stone surrounded by artificial flowers. It commemorates one of Scotland's greatest music-hall entertainers, the great [2] WILL FYFFE (1885-1947). The Dundee-born actor, singer

and comedian was the son of a shipyard worker and part-time theatrical entrepreneur. As a young character actor Will toured Scotland playing Shakespeare, an early training in diction, timing and characterisation that prepared him well for his future great success treading the boards of Scotland's variety theatres, performing his own inimitable compositions, 'Sailing up the Clyde', 'She was the Belle of the Ball' and most memorably, 'I belong to Glasgow.' He also appeared in more than 23 films. Tragically, Will Fyffe died in St Andrews in an accident following an operation.

And now let us move on to the odd-man-out in this guide because, although his dust belongs forever here, he has no grave in the Western Necropolis, nor in any other Glasgow graveyard. In life as well as death he was considered odd.

BRITANNIA MUSIC HALL,
COURTESY OF THE
RCAHMS

A Yorkshire man [3] ALBERT ERNEST PICKARD (d1964, aged 90) came to Glasgow in the early 1900s. He bought the derelict Britannia Music Hall in the Trongate and turned it into Glasgow's favourite variety theatre. Stan Laurel and Jack Buchanan made their first public performances at this theatre which Pickard re-named 'The Panopticon'.

The 'Go-As-You-Please' competitions he ran — singing, dancing, conjuring, acrobatics — were glorious fun for those in the audience and a horrific running-of-the-gauntlet for the

COURTESY OF THE RCAHMS

competitors. Not one aspiring artiste left the stage without being plastered with rotten fruit! Pickard also arranged strange exhibitions to fascinate his customers, sometimes even displaying shrunken human heads.

He was a rich man and owned a Kilmarnock Edition of the poems of Robert Burns which cost him £800. He also owned the world's largest teapot, more than three feet tall, made of white porcelain. Later he bought cinemas. His 'White Elephant' in Shawlands was considered more posh than the 'Black Cat' in Parkhead which had a legendary resident flea called *Rosie*.

It is said that one day Pickard went onto the site of a cinema being built for one of his competitors. He asked a crane driver to lend him a pound. A pound would have been almost a week's wages, so the crane-driver told Pickard, 'By the look of that limousine of yours standing at the gate, it's more likely you could lend me a pound'. Pickard said, 'Give me a pound and you can have the limousine!' Those who best knew this grand eccentric, claimed that he would have done such a deal, although the crane-driver was not convinced enough to come up with the pound. Pickard also stood in a General Election as 'Independent Millionaire for Maryhill'. How bitterly he resented losing his deposit.

Tragically, Albert Pickard died in a fire at his Great Western Road mansion one Hallowe'en. His body was brought to the Western Necropolis crematorium and his ashes were scattered in the Garden of Remembrance.

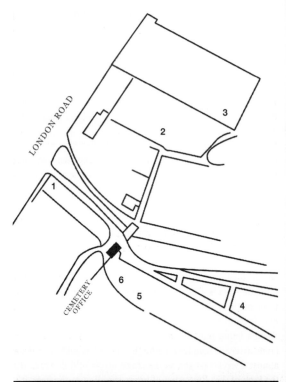

LONDON ROAD

3

2

1

CEMETERY
OFFICE

6

5

4

St Peter's Cemetery (Dalbeth)

1900 London Road, GLASGOW G32 8XG
Tel: 0141 778 1183

To find St Peter's, head east along Gallowgate from Glasgow Cross into London Road. There is about a four-mile journey along this road (which, incidentally, ultimately reaches London), passing the famous Barras Market on the left, and, further on, Celtic Park at Parkhead and the 2012 Commonwealth Games facilities opposite on the right. About 200 metres on the right beyond Dewars, the whisky

distillers, turn into St Peter's Cemetery. The cemetery has been here since 1851 and is on the fringe of a place celebrated in song and story – Auchenshuggle.

Visitors would hardly expect to find a graveyard in the East End of Glasgow complete with lines of ornate stone angels, flowers and trees. There are no concessions towards staid Calvinism here – with one exception. Just inside the main gate, turn sharply right, and in the corner by the wall, against a fence, is a large broad granite stone with, at each side, a classic fluted column in relief. The Doric capitals on the columns of this stone have no French or Italian overtones.

Labour MP [1] JOHN WHEATLEY (1869-1930) is buried here. As Minister of Health in the Labour Government of 1924, his Housing Act provided new municipal houses in clean, bright estates at rents working people could afford. Thousands moved out of the old city tenements to begin a new way of living.

JOHN WHEATLEY, COURTESY OF MRS KATHLEEN DALYELL

The old method of achieving a full-body wash by crouching in a tin tub in front of the kitchen fire, became a bad memory. The new houses had enamel baths in bathrooms with toilets!

Wheatley was an Irish Catholic from County Wexford. His father came to Scotland to work in a pit at Bargeddie and

John followed on to become a miner. He was a bright lad – night-classes at the Glasgow Athenaeum were his escape from the pit. He worked in a pub, a grocer's shop, sold advertising for *The Glasgow Observer*, and then went into partnership in a printing firm. But his personality was such that he was destined to become a politician.

Rent increases during World War I led to the famous Glasgow Rent Strike. He was then a Glasgow councillor and joined battle with the authorities to prevent the eviction of Mrs McHugh of Shettleston who couldn't pay her rent. Her soldier husband had been badly wounded in France.

Wheatley won popular support and stopped the eviction. Indeed, his action prompted Lloyd George to introduce his Rent Restriction Bill and rents were thus pegged for the duration of the War. However, Wheatley's political activities meant an uneasy relationship for him with the Catholic hierarchy. It sometimes flared into open warfare.

Oddly enough, he was not given a Cabinet position in the Labour Government of 1929 and in the early months of 1930, his health began to deteriorate. Years of stress were taking their toll. He died in Shettleston, his home and parliamentary constituency, late on a May night after travelling from Birmingham.

On the day of his funeral, thousands of local and well known people alike came together to bid farewell to their champion. Neville Chamberlain, with whom John had often crossed swords in Parliament, came to pay tribute to a much-respected opponent. Oswald Mosley, later to lead the British Fascist *Blackshirts*, stood by the grave. Beside them was the Revd Dr John White, Moderator of the General Assembly of the Church of Scotland, who also came to mark his respect for a fellow Christian. It is just a pity that the fine headstone above his grave has been robbed of the portrait head it once displayed!

Continue down the path from the main gate until you reach a flight of stairs on the left. Go up the stairs and along a path. This leads to what was once the 'Good Shepherd' part of the graveyard, with a primary school and a church.

From 1865 the Good Shepherd order of nuns ran a reformatory for girls, not far from the Catholic Boys Reformatory at West Thorn Mills on the west side of Dalbeth Burn. However, the Good Shepherd Sisters left Dalbeth in 1949 and the parish (established in 1948) closed in 1975 and the church was taken down. The primary school was also closed and most of the complex of buildings eventually demolished.

Go down the road towards the Cemetery Office (on the right). Opposite the office turn left up the flight of steps where you can see the marker for Section 7. Go around 100 paces along a wooden fence: just as the path veers right (near a notice for Section 3) continue instead into the graveyard ahead of you. Immediately you will come to a tall, grey, granite stone facing away from you. Here is the grave of the masterly Scottish footballer [2] JIMMY McGRORY (d1982, aged 78).

JIMMY MCGRORY,
COURTESY OF THE
CARRUTH FAMILY

McGrory was a Celtic legend in his own time. An old-fashioned centre forward, he looked like a strong man in a circus, with his thick neck and bullet-like head. He represented Scotland in 13 internationals, but it was that head which made him a legend. It could target the ball into the net from two inches or ten feet above the pitch! And from impossible angles! The energy he transmitted to the ball turned it into a missile that even hands like shovels could not deflect!

On the terracing Celtic fans wrote their own folk songs about him. Old men playing dominoes in pubs, still hum those songs, and smile, as they lay down the double-six.

They didn't think of him as being 78 years old when they laid him to rest here in 1982. To them he was still the boy with the *rocket header*!

Step back onto the path you were walking on before and walk on till you reach the high stone wall of Old Dalbeth Cemetery. Over the wall you can see the backs of monuments known as the 'Bishops' Ground', part of the old Dalbeth cemetery.

PRIESTS' MONUMENT

Here, among the priests whose names are inscribed on six marble panels set into an ornate and broad stone structure, lies [6] Father PATRICK McLAUGHLIN (d1895, aged 73). In 1853 this Irish priest built the first Catholic church in the area at Eastmuir. It was a timber hut. Eastmuir was only a small part of Shettleston. Father McLaughlin's parish of some 3,000 souls was spread over a huge area east of the city, extending from the River Clyde almost to the Campsie Hills in the north. He was popular with the whole community because he offered help to those who needed it without asking which religion they followed. When he visited sick people in the dead of night, wrapped in his shepherd's cloak, local miners along the way, Protestant and Catholic alike, used their pit-lamps to light his path.

While he was in charge at Shettleston, a thief, with remorse of conscience, came to Father McLaughlin's confessional and owned up to his crime. He returned the good priest the money he had stolen. Father McLaughlin wrote down on an envelope the name and address of the person from whom the money had been taken, and the cash was returned to its rightful owner.

Unfortunately, the police traced the handwriting on the envelope to the parish priest and demanded that he reveal the name of the culprit. Father McLaughlin repeatedly refused, saying that he could never divulge what had been said to him by anyone in the confessional. He was charged and sentenced to 30 days in Duke Street Jail for obstructing the police. But he served only 14. Bishop John Murdoch of Glasgow intervened and leniency was shown. His return to Shettleston was a triumphal procession. An open carriage conveyed him along a route lined with cheering admirers – of all creeds and of none!

He died in Rothesay after five years of retirement. No matter what type of society he had been born into, Patrick McLaughlin would have been that special kind of creature – a good and honest man.

Go back to the Cemetery Office. Then turn left and walk forward past the notice for Section 3B. Go across the grass past 12 gravestones. Now you will see a sombre heavy obelisk. On the faces of this stone in Section 9 are inscribed the names of 61 of over 200 [5] MINERS, who died on 22 October 1877.   On that day, the small town of Blantyre in Lanarkshire was rocked with the shock waves of a mighty explosion. The people of the town knew immediately what had happened. The devastating blast had come from the bowels of the local Blantyre Ferme Pit. Terror swept through the town as families rushed to the pithead. Before long, the horror they feared was confirmed – over 200 men had died. The 61 miners who perished and are remembered at Dalbeth were all Catholics. The stone displays the names – the youngest, 13-year-old PETER BURNS ... the oldest, 59-year-old NEIL WARD. This stone tells us about the real price of coal.

Walk back to the Section 3B notice and then turn left, going right over to the long hedge. Here you will see the imposing monument to the [3] GREEN family and to GEORGE GREEN (d1915, aged 54), the foremost pioneer of the cinema in Glasgow. He opened his picture houses in the early years of the 20th century when people said the moving picture was but a passing fad.

Green's sons George and Herbert kept the 'flicks' flickering. They built up their cinema empire which extended from the humble Tollcross Cinema – known locally,
and affectionately, as 'The Scum' – to the magnificent Green's Playhouse in Renfield Street, the largest cinema in Europe, with seating for 4400 patrons.

Lads took their girlfriends to the plush red divans in the Playhouse at one shilling and sixpence a ticket – or, if funds allowed, to the golden divans at two bob each! Above the cinema, the ballroom accommodated hundreds of dancers jiving to the dance bands of Joe Loss or Oscar Rabin.

George Jnr, more often called by his middle name Fred, went to Hollywood on many occasions. He made friends with Charlie Chaplin. He must have had many wonderful memories to enjoy in his latter years. He died in 1965, aged 78. His mother, Ann, is in this lair, and also his sister, Veronica, the wife of that fabulous footballer whose grave you have just visited – Jimmy McGrory.

In front of the hedge, in this same line of memorials, 13 stones along from the Greens, look for the grave of [4] Sir PATRICK DOLLAN (d1963, aged 77).

Paddy Dollan's first claim to fame was staked when he served as an altar boy at John Wheatley's wedding in Baillieston. He was a smart lad who educated himself out of the pits. Following a career in politics, he eventually became Lord Provost of Glasgow from 1938 to

1941. He later headed the East Kilbride New Town Development Corporation.

In his early days as a political agitator, he once suggested to his fellow miners that they should demand pit-head baths. They thought Paddy was insulting them! How dare he question their personal hygiene! They chased him for his life!

During the Empire Exhibition at Bellahouston Park in 1938, Sir Patrick had the job, as Lord Provost and first citizen, of accompanying visiting celebrities to the big show. Unfortunately he was a man with a grave demeanour, and his voice sometimes had a sepulchre-like timbre to it. These characteristics had the crowd in stitches at the Bellahouston bandstand as he gloomily introduced the world-

COURTESY OF THE DOLLAN FAMILY

famous Hollywood comedian, Eddie Cantor, to the audience. The crowd demanded a song from Eddie, who went into a funny routine with his classic '*If you knew Suzie like I know Suzie ... Oh! ... Oh! ... Oh, what a Gal!*' While the comedian danced around Paddy, the Lord Provost remained immobile and dreary of countenance, and the crowds hooted all the harder. However, in all fairness, Paddy Dollan made good use of his 77 years improving the lot of his fellow man.

139

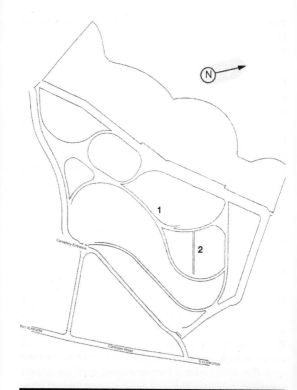

Cathcart Cemetery

East Renfrewshire Council, 160 Brenfield Road,
Cathcart, Glasgow G44 3JW
Tel: 0141 577 3913

Formerly inside the boundaries of the City of Glasgow, since local government reorganisation in 1996 Cathcart has been part of East Renfrewshire. From Argyle Street, the route is south, down Stockwell Street, over the Clyde, into Gorbals Street and on to Cathcart Road. After about two miles, turn left into Holmlea Road which eventually becomes Clarkston Road. Turn left into Clarkston Road and look out for the graveyard straight ahead at the T-junction with Brenfield Road.

Through the main gate, a wide forecourt stretches in front of a boarded-up lodge house. Take the road to the left and continue round a long sweeping curve which rises as it goes. Where it begins to level off, the small M Section of the graveyard is on the left.

At the end of the section, an area is fenced off for refuse collection. Pass it, then look out now on the left side of the

road at the first line of gravestones right on the edge of the road. Unhappily, the ravages of time have seen this stone fall flat on its face. Nevertheless, here is the gravestone of the [1] MACKIE family. This is the L Section and the Mackie stone is marked L204. The unmarked grave to the left of it is lair L203.

In this grave lies a professional singer called MADGE METCALFE. She was buried here in December 1908, aged 50, still in her prime. The records state that she died of 'debility'.

Madge Metcalfe's married name was Jefferson. Her husband Arthur, a native of Ulverston in Cumbria, brought his family to Glasgow in 1901 after a stay in Bishop Auckland. A man of the theatre, he became manager of the Scotia Music Hall in Stockwell Street, later known as the 'Metropole'.

The Jefferson son, Stanley, couldn't wait to slap on the greasepaint and get out in front of the footlights. He fancied himself as a singer, dancer and light comedian. But no amount of pleading would persuade Arthur Jefferson to give his son a spot in the show.

Undeterred, 16-year-old Stanley went along to the rival Panopticon in Argyle Street and asked its owner, AE Pickard (whom we have already met) for a job. Pickard said 'yes' and young Stanley had his first-ever professional performance. He was a smash hit! And there was to be no looking back. And thus the showbiz career of one Stan Laurel, complete with new stage name, took off. This was many years, of course, before the immortal pairing of Stan Laurel with Oliver Hardy.

Questions still linger over the grave of Stan Laurel's mother. Why was no stone ever set here to mark her final resting-place? Did the great Hollywood star ever get a chance to stand for a quiet moment or two at her graveside during his fleeting visit to Glasgow in 1932 or later in the 1950s, mobbed by cheering fans. Why, as it seems, was she forgotten?

Move on along this road to a point where it divides into three narrower roads. Go up the middle one up to the top of the hill. On your right is the O Section.

Turn right and walk down a grassy path to the fourth line of gravestones on your left. There you will find a large, wide, granite stone facing the path you are on. Here rest the [2] McCOLLS. The most famous was ROBERT S McCOLL (d1958, aged 82). He played amateur football with Queens Park, but he was so good that Newcastle United snapped him up and made him a professional. But he was still with Queens Park when he earned his first international cap in March 1896 against Wales, aged 20. He won 13 full caps in all. After Newcastle he joined Rangers Football Club, earning the title of 'King of all centre-forwards'. However, in the 1906-07 season he astonished the football world by returning to the amateur ranks with his old club, Queens Park.

Football was not Bob McColl's only claim to fame. He and his brother, Thomas, who also lies here, must have sensed that there was profit to be made exploiting Glasgow's notorious sweet tooth. So they opened a 'sweetie' factory.

In Scotland (and especially in Glasgow) confections are never called just 'sweets' or 'candy' – sweets in this city are given exotic names, from

ROBERT S MCCOLL,
COURTESY OF THE
RCAHMS

'conversation lozenges' to 'chocolate drops' or 'hazelnut whirls'. The McColls opened shops to retail their luscious joys. In the days when cinema-going was a main Glasgow pastime, few patrons would think about going into the box-office without first dropping in at RS McColl's for a poke of sweeties. Even the addict would keep some back for the 'big' picture.

Perhaps Glasgow dentists ought to get together sometime to arrange a pilgrimage to the McColl grave, by way of giving thanks for the business the sweetie-sooking McColl customers must have put their way.

Bibliography

Barr, William W, *Glaswegiana*
(Glasgow: Vista, 1972)

Berry, James J., *The Glasgow Necropolis Heritage Trail*
(Glasgow: Bell and Bain Ltd., 1985, reprinted 1987)

Cowan, James, *From Glasgow's Treasure Chest*
(Glasgow: Craig Wilson, 1951)

Glasgow's Glasgow, *People within a City*
(Glasgow: The Words and the Stones, 1990)

Hutt, Charlotte, *City of the Dead*
(Glasgow: Glasgow City Libraries and Archives, 1996)

Johnston, Ruth *Glasgow Necropolis*
(Glasgow: Johnstondesign, 2006)

Mackenzie, Peter, *Old Reminiscences and Remarkable Characters of Glasgow* (Glasgow: James P Forrester 1875)

Miller, Susan and Fairie, J Scott, *Glasgow Cathedral New Burying Ground*
(Glasgow: Glasgow and West of Scotland Family History Society, 2004)

Scott, Ronnie, *Death by Design*
(Edinburgh: Black and White Publishing, 2005)

Simpson, William, *Glasgow in the 'Forties*
(Glasgow: Morison Brothers, 1899)

Smart, Andy, *Old Springburn, Glasgow:*
Richard Stenlake, 1982)

Turnbull, Michael TRB, *The Edinburgh Graveyard Guide*
(Saint Andrew Press, 1991; Scottish Cultural Press, 2006)

Waugh, Thomas M, *Shettleston from Old and New Photographs* (Sandyhill East Community Council, 1986)

Willing, June A and Fairie, J Scott, *Burial Grounds of Glasgow*
(Glasgow and West of Scotland Family History Society, 1986)

Access, Contacts and Administration

GLASGOW CITY COUNCIL
Cemeteries & Crematoria Registrar
20 Trongate
GLASGOW G1 5ES
Tel: 0141 287 3961

Glasgow Cathedral
Castle Street
GLASGOW G4 0QZ
Cathedral Office
Tel: 0141 552 8198
Historic Scotland
Tel: 0141 552 6891

Glasgow Necropolis
70 Cathedral Square
GLASGOW G4 0UZ

Calton Burying Ground
Abercromby Street
GLASGOW G40 1NQ

Gorbals Cemetery
Commercial Road
GLASGOW G5 0RG

Sighthill Cemetery
300 Springburn Road
GLASGOW G21 1SE

Southern Necropolis
300 Caledonia Road
GLASGOW G5 0TB

St Kentigern's
951 Balmore Road
GLASGOW G23 5AA

Western Necropolis
19 Tresta Road
GLASGOW G23 5AA

ARCHDIOCESE OF GLASGOW
St. Peter's Dalbeth
1900 London Road
GLASGOW G32 8XG
Tel: 0141 778 1183

STRATHCLYDE UNIVERSITY
St David's (Ramshorn) Kirk,
98 Ingram Street
GLASGOW G1 1ES
Tel: 0141 548 2542

EAST RENFREWSHIRE COUNCIL
Cathcart Cemetery
160 Brenfield Road
CATHCART G44 3JW
Tel: 0141 577 3913

Useful Addresses

Glasgow City Council
Land and Environment Services (LES)
231 George Street,
GLASGOW
G1 1RX
Tel: 0141 287 5064 (minimum of six people per tour or walk)
Email: les@glasgow.gov.uk

The Friends of Glasgow Necropolis
Cathedral House Hotel,
28/32 Cathedral Square,
GLASGOW G4 0XA
Email: enquiries@glasgownecropolis.org
www.glasgownecropolis.org

Southern Necropolis Heritage Trail
www.southernnecropolis.com

City of the Dead Guide to Glasgow's Southern Necropolis:
www.glasgow.gov.uk/en/Residents/Parks_Outdoors/HeritageTrails
/SouthernNecropolis/southernnecropolisheritagetrail5to8.htm

Scottish Jewish Archive Centre
129 Hill Street
Garnethill
GLASGOW
G3 6UB
Tel: 0141 332 4911
Email: info@sjac.org.uk
www.sjac.org.uk

Index

ABBREVIATIONS

Calton = C
Cathcart Cemetery = CC
Glasgow Cathedral interior = GC interior
Glasgow Cathedral new churchyard = GCnc
Glasgow Cathedral old churchyard = GCoc
Glasgow Necropolis = GN
Jocelyn Square = JS
Saint David's Burying Ground (Ramshorn Kirk) = SDR
Saint David's Crypt (Ramshorn Kirk) = SDRC
Saint Kentigern's = SK
Saint Peter's Dalbeth = SPD
Sighthill = S
Southern Necropolis = SN
Western Necropolis = WN

Provand, Andrew Dryburgh (MP: SDR) 80-1

Rainy, Harry (surgeon: GCnc) 35
Reid, Hugh (engineer: GN) 66
Reid, Neil (bricklayer: GCnc) 31
Reston, James (soldier: SN) 101
Riddell, William (contractor: GCnc) 36
Risk, Forrest (S) 90-1
Risk, Margaret (S) 90-1
Robb, William (SN) 109
Robertson, John (engineer: SN) 105-6
Rodger, Alexander (weaver: GN) 46
Roger, George Jr (GCoc) 18
Roxburgh, John (minister: GCnc) 33-4

Smart, James (superintendent: SN) 103-4
Smith, Alexander (slater: GCoc) 17
Smith, James (minister: C) 116
Smith, James Elishama (minister: SN) 103
Smith, Magdalene (SN) 108-9
Smith, William (Boys Brigade founder: WN) 128-9
Stillborn children, memorial to (GN entrance) 42

Taylor, John (weaver: GCoc) 16
Tennant, Charles (industrialist: GN) 68-9
Tennent, Charles SP (brewer: GN) 50
Tennent family (brewers: GN) 13-4, 50-1
Tennent, Hugh (brewer: GCoc) 13
Thomson, Alexander (architect: SN) 109-10
Thomson, Charles (musician: SN) 110
Thomson, William (scientist: GN) 54-5

Victoria Cross, memorial to those awarded (GN entrance) 42

Ward, Neil (miner: SPD) 137
Wardlaw, Ralph (minister: GN) 59-60
Watson, George Lennox (naval architect: GN) 49
Wheatley, John (MP: SPD) 133-4
White, Willie (street performer: SN) 111
Wilson, John (G) 120-1
Wilson, Dr William Rae (solicitor: GN) 69-70

Graveyard Log

		Date Visited	Remarks

Glasgow Cathedral

		Date Visited	Remarks
1	Saint Kentigern		
2	Dame Margaret Colquhoun		
3	Orr Family		
4	Moses McCulloch		
5	Richard Dennistoun		
6	Kirkman Finlay		

Glasgow Cathedral old churchyard

		Date Visited	Remarks
1	George Baillie		
2	George Hutcheson		
	Thomas Hutcheson		
3	Hugh Tennent & family		
4	Colin Dunlop Donald		
5	James McCall		
6	Margaret Balmanno		
7	John Taylor		
	John Andrew		
8	A. McKxAB		
9	Alexander Smith		
10	MacIntosh family		
11	Charles MacIntosh		
12	George Roger, Jnr		
13	Bells of Cowcaddens		
14	Mary Hill		
15	Robert Maxwell		

		Date Visited	Remarks
	Patrick Maxwell		
	Bessy Boyd		
16	John George Hamilton		
17	Peter Murdoch		
18	Peter Low		
19	Mrs Hamilton of Aitkenhead		
20	Revd John Burns		
21	Andrew Menzies		
22	Alexander Cowan		
23	James Campbell		
24	William Bogle		
25	Andrew Buchanan		

Glasgow Cathedral new churchyard

		Date Visited	Remarks
1	Robert Easton		
2	Maxwell family		
3	Neil Reid		
4	Dr William Chrystal		
5	Antonio Galletti		
6	David Hamilton		
7	Revd John Roxburgh		
8	William McKenzie		
9	James McOran		
10	Dr Harry Rainey		
11	William Riddell		

Glasgow Necropolis

Entrance Memorials

A   Stillborn children

B   Victoria Cross

C   Korean War

1   William Harper Minnoch

2   Charles William Fry

3   James Mitchell

4   Alexander Rodger

5   Alexander McCall

6   Hugh Percy Forster

7   Robert Heckmann

8   John Bell

9   George Lennox Watson

10   John McDonald

11   Tennent family

12   Alexander Mackenzie

13   François Foucart

14   Major Archibald D Monteath

15   Lt-Col Alexander Hope Pattison

16   Dr Granville Sharp Pattison

17   William Thomson, Lord Kelvin

18   William Miller

19   James Davidson

20   Aitkens of Dalmoak

		Date Visited	Remarks
21	William McGavin		
22	Lt Joseph Gomoszynski		
23	Peter Mackenzie		
24	William Dunn		
25	Eliza Jane Aikman		
26	Revd Ralph Wardlaw		
27	Henry Monteith		
28	John Henry Alexander		
29	Dugald Moore		
30	Revd Duncan MacFarlan		
31	James Ewing		
32	Sir James Lumsden		
33	Robert Baird		
34	John Elder		
35	Professors of Glasgow University		
36	Glasgow Fire Brigade		
	Glasgow Salvage Corps		
37	Sir Hugh Reid		
38	Alexander Allan		
39	Revd George Matheson		
40	Walter MacFarlane		
41	Henry Dubs		
42	John Houldsworth		
43	Charles Tennant		
44	Dr William Rae Wilson		

		Date Visited	Remarks
45	Revd Alexander Ogilvie Beattie	_____	_____
46	Hugh Cogan	_____	_____
47	William Motherwell	_____	_____
48	Catherine Black	_____	_____
49	Corinda Lee	_____	_____
50	Jewish Cemetery	_____	_____

St David's Burying Ground (Ramshorn Kirk)

		Date Visited	Remarks
1	Andrew Foulis	_____	_____
	Robert Foulis	_____	_____
2	Glassford family	_____	_____
3	Robert Carrick	_____	_____
4	David McQuater	_____	_____
5	Monteith family	_____	_____
6	William Friend Durant	_____	_____
7	Revd James Fisher	_____	_____
8	Alexander Glen	_____	_____
9	Fleming family	_____	_____
10	Pierre Émile L'Angelier	_____	_____
11	Provand family	_____	_____
12	David Dale	_____	_____

St David's Crypt (Ramshorn Kirk)

		Date Visited	Remarks
1	James Darnley	_____	_____
2	Alex Broom	_____	_____
3	Dr James Cleland	_____	_____

	Date Visited	Remarks

Sighthill Cemetery

#	Name	Date Visited	Remarks
1	Robert Curle	_____	_____
2	Martyr's Monument	_____	_____
3	John Milne Donald	_____	_____
4	Forrest & Margaret Risk	_____	_____
5	Mossman family	_____	_____
6	James Hedderick	_____	_____
7	Benjamin Connor	_____	_____
8	Revd James Aitcheson Johnston	_____	_____
9	James Moir	_____	_____
10	Mackenzie Murdoch	_____	_____
11	James Laurie	_____	_____
12	Professor William Leiper	_____	_____
	William Leiper	_____	_____

Southern Necropolis

#	Name	Date Visited	Remarks
1	Revd Nathaniel Paterson	_____	_____
2	Peter Ferguson	_____	_____
3	Sir Thomas Lipton	_____	_____
4	Sergeant James Reston	_____	_____
	Agnes Harkness	_____	_____
5	John Begg	_____	_____
6	Revd James Elishama Smith	_____	_____
7	Superintendent James Smart	_____	_____
8	Hugh MacDonald	_____	_____
9	John Robertson	_____	_____

	Date Visited	Remarks
3 Albert Ernest Pickard	_____	_____

St Peter's Cemetery (Dalbeth)

1 John Wheatley	_____	_____
2 Jimmy McGrory	_____	_____
3 Father Patrick McLaughlin	_____	_____
4 Miners' memorial	_____	_____
5 Green family	_____	_____
6 Sir Patrick Dollan	_____	_____

Cathcart Cemetery

1 Mackie family	_____	_____
Madge Metcalfe	_____	_____
2 McColl family	_____	_____